MW00773703

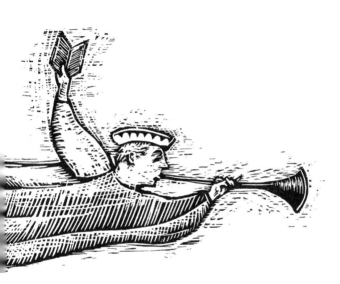

Helaman: *a brief theological introduction*

This publication was made possible by generous support from the Laura F. Willes Center for Book of Mormon Studies, part of the Neal A. Maxwell Institute for Religious Scholarship at Brigham Young University.

Published by the Neal A. Maxwell Institute for Religious Scholarship, Brigham Young University, Provo, Utah. The copyright for the 2013 text of The Book of Mormon is held by The Church of Jesus Christ of Latter-day Saints, Salt Lake City, Utah; that text is quoted throughout and used by permission.

Printed in the United States of America

ISBN: 978-0-8425-0019-7

LIBRARY OF CONGRESS CONTROL NUMBER: 2020902549

# Helaman

*a brief theological introduction*

BRIGHAM YOUNG UNIVERSITY

NEAL A. MAXWELL INSTITUTE

PROVO, UTAH

Kimberly Matheson Berkey

*The Book of Mormon: brief theological introductions* series seeks Christ in scripture by combining intellectual rigor and the disciple's yearning for holiness. It answers Elder Neal A. Maxwell's call to explore the book's "divine architecture": "There is so much more in the Book of Mormon than we have yet discovered. The book's divine architecture and rich furnishings will increasingly unfold to our view, further qualifying it as *'a marvelous work and a wonder.'* (Isaiah 29:14) . . . All the rooms in this mansion need to be explored, whether by valued traditional scholars or by those at the cutting edge. Each plays a role, and one LDS scholar cannot say to the other, *'I have no need of thee.'"* [1] (1 Corinthians 12:21)

For some time, faithful scholars have explored the book's textual history, reception, historicity, literary quality, and more. This series focuses particularly on theology—the scholarly practice of exploring a scriptural text's implications and its lens on God's work in the world. Series volumes invite Latter-day Saints to discover additional dimensions of this treasured text but leave to prophets and apostles their unique role of declaring its definitive official doctrines. In this case, theology, as opposed to authoritative doctrine, relates to the original sense of the term as, literally, reasoned "God talk." The word also designates a well-developed academic field, but it is the more general sense of the term that most often applies here. By engaging each scriptural book's theology on its own terms, this series explores the spiritual and intellectual force of the ideas appearing in the Latter-day Saints' "keystone" scripture.

Series authors and editors possess specialized professional training that informs their work but, significantly, each takes Christ as theology's proper end because he is the proper end of all scripture and all reflection on it. We, too, "talk of Christ, we rejoice in Christ, we preach of Christ . . . that our children may know to what source they may look for a remission of their sins" (2 Nephi 25:26). Moreover, while experts in the modern disciplines of philosophy, theology, literature, and history, series authors and editors also work explicitly within the context of personal and institutional commitments both to Christian discipleship and to The Church of Jesus Christ of Latter-day Saints. These volumes are not official Church publications but can be best understood in light of these deep commitments. And because we acknowledge that scripture demands far more than intellectual experimentation, we call readers' attention to the processes of conversion and sanctification at play on virtually every scriptural page.

Individual series authors offer unique approaches but, taken together, they model a joint invitation to readers to engage scripture in their own way. No single approach to theology or scriptural interpretation commands preeminence in these volumes. No volume pretends to be the final word on theological reflection for its part of the Book of Mormon. Varied perspectives and methodologies are evident throughout. This is intentional. In addition, though we recognize love for the Book of Mormon is a "given" for most Latter-day Saint readers, we also share the conviction that, like the gospel of Jesus Christ itself, the Book of Mormon is inexhaustible.[2] These volumes invite readers to slow down and read scripture more thoughtfully and transformatively. Elder Maxwell cautioned against reading the Book of Mormon as "hurried tourists" who scarcely venture beyond "the entry hall."[3] To that end, we dedicate this series to his apostolic conviction that there is always more to learn from the Book of Mormon and much to be gained from our faithful search for Christ in its pages.
　—The Editors

# Contents

# Introduction

The book of Helaman is a slim volume, relatively brief and easily overlooked. Only sixteen chapters long and covering just fifty years of the Book of Mormon's millennium-length narrative, this sliver of a text is squeezed by the prestige of the book on either side. Helaman ☛ doesn't have the impressive heft or sermonic richness of Alma and is often overshadowed by the climactic arrival of Jesus in 3 Nephi. Understandably, readers thus tend to construe it as either an afterword to the wars of the preceding book or an explanatory preamble to the book that follows. Our relative neglect of Helaman, however, is unwarranted. This is the book where secret combinations first show up narratively and where we hear from the Book of Mormon's only Lamanite prophet, and it is the first time in the large plates when Nephite destruction is portended in full. Helaman's pages contain the first murder of a chief judge, Mormon's most extended and poetic interlude (Hel. 12), and the only scene that comes anywhere close to rivaling the theophany in 3 Nephi (Hel. 5). Between the obscurity in which most readers have left it and the overwhelming richness of what lies buried within its pages, Helaman is easily one of the best-kept secrets of the Book of Mormon.

☛ When I use the word "Helaman" by itself I am referring to the book of Helaman not the person Helaman. When I refer to Helaman the person, I will use subscripts to differentiate Helaman son of Alma (Helaman$_1$) from Helaman son of Helaman (Helaman$_2$). The Book of Mormon also includes one other person named Helaman, a son of King Benjamin (Mosiah 1:2). However, as he is not mentioned in this book (nor anywhere in the series), he is not included in the subscript numbering. Similarly, subscripts distinguish people with the same name through this book (and the series): Nephi, Mosiah, Alma, etc.

Three notes will prepare our reading of this extraordinary text: a word on political motivation, a word on structure, and a word on theme. We need to grapple with what readers usually expect to find in Helaman, the careful organization of what they actually find there, and the lessons that lie on the other side of that reading.

### politics and the book of Helaman

First, politically speaking, it's important to acknowledge that most readers come to Helaman having just waded through over two hundred pages of political wrangling in the books of Mosiah and Alma. Between the merger of three different political and religious entities (Mosiah 25), the new status and organization given to the church (Mosiah 26), and the transition from a monarchy to a system of judges (Mosiah 29), the Nephites are left at the end of Mosiah with a number of unreconciled tensions that fuel every major conflict to come. From this point on, Nephite dissenters become a regular feature of Book of Mormon politics. Almost as soon as the system of judges is instituted, the book of Alma reports attempt after attempt to undermine the new law, headed by figures such as Amlici, Nehor, and the long string of Nehor's followers. These tensions ultimately lead to an extended war that consumes the second half of the book. Though some of these political priorities go underground in the meanwhile, they reemerge with a vengeance as soon as peace is restored.

Readers are plenty familiar with the political tone of this stretch of the Nephite story. What's more, they know that the book of Helaman will only ramp up that theme: partisan assassinations, secret plots for power, and government corruption are about to become regular features of the narrative. Naturally, then—and rightly!—readers come to Helaman on the lookout for the Book of Mormon's next political development. Quite naturally, too, as faithful Latter-day Saints they look to the political tensions of this book as a guide to the political tensions of their own communities and nations. Because Mosiah and Alma prime us to read Helaman politically, and because we trust in the Book of Mormon as a spiritual guide for our lives, we tend to run headlong into the text assuming that we will find implications for governments, political parties, democracy, election procedures, international relations, and every other institution we associate with the exercise of power.

These are good impulses; for one thing, they cause us to take seriously the Book of Mormon's implications for our lives and pay attention to the developments that prove so pivotal for the Nephites' fate. Unfortunately, however, these impulses also lead us to overlook what Helaman hopes to show us. It is a deeply political text, yes, and it contains lessons about the exercise of power, but the questions Helaman poses about these topics are not the questions readers tend to ask when they come to the book. What's important is not *that* secret combinations emerge but *how*; not *that* there are corrupt plots in the highest levels of government but *how* the Nephites overlook their own role in nurturing that corruption; not *that* their society collapses but *how* they blind themselves to the process.

The book of Helaman has too often been subject to a well-intentioned but ultimately blind hunt for contemporary political parallels without regard for their interpretive warrant or their historical basis (something biblical scholars refer to as *parallelomania*). Seeing secret combinations at work among the Nephites, readers begin to look for secret combinations in their own governments. Reading alarming narratives about political assassinations, they narrow their eyes suspiciously whenever a prominent public figure dies. Warned that conspiracies will be widespread in the last days, they become conspiracy theorists, secure in the idea that they are heeding Helaman's counsel to guard against hidden threats. Though there is always warrant for being attentive to current events, the book of Helaman is not a set of ready-made labels to be applied at will to modern political situations (always a risky endeavor, anyway, when working across hundreds of years of historical and cultural difference). Rather, readers are encouraged to watch for the spiritual conditions in their own hearts, families, and communities that allow these phenomena to take root in the first place. Though I will say more about the themes of Helaman in a moment, this much is clear: readers who come to this book expecting justification to identify "secret combinations" among their political opponents or an endorsement of anxieties about political conspiracies will be sorely disappointed. The lesson of Helaman is not that we must ramp up our sense of threat in the political arena but rather that we are lousy at recognizing what truly threatens us in the first place.

*the structure of the book of Helaman*

Second, we need to note the deliberate care with which this book is structured. Mormon is clearly up to something when he switches from Alma to Helaman. For instance, readers will notice a sudden increase in the speed of the story. Though the book of Alma dedicates sixty-three chapters to covering a period of forty years, Helaman spends only a fraction of that space covering an even longer stretch of time (sixteen chapters to cover fifty years). Readers may even feel relieved at this sudden uptick in pace; sick of political intrigue, tired of hearing about endless wars, and annoyed by the minutia of troop movements, we're ready for things to move along. But Mormon is not getting bored or running out of space; he's doing this on purpose. He has a specific story to tell, and it requires a specific shape as well as a specific tempo.

The 1830 edition of the Book of Mormon did not have the same chapter breaks that Latter-day Saint readers are accustomed to today. When Joseph Smith originally dictated the record, he not only designated the words of the text but also instructed his scribes on where to insert breaks between chapters. Though the current LDS edition of the Book of Mormon no longer honors these divisions (mostly because of their length), they are part of the original Book of Mormon text and, for believers, reflect the  organizational priorities of the book's original editors (Nephi, Mormon, and Moroni). In that 1830 edition, the book of Helaman had five original chapters. What we call chapters 1–2 were gathered into a single unit, the original chapter I, followed by our chapters 3–6 as the original chapter II, and so on. The entire book of Helaman was grouped as follows:

| | |
|---|---|
| Chapter I | Helaman 1–2 |
| Chapter II | Helaman 3–6 |
| Chapter III | Helaman 7–10 |
| Chapter IV | Helaman 11–12 |
| Chapter V | Helaman 13–16 |

Furthermore, each of these original chapters has an obvious narrative coherence. The original chapter I recounts the rise of secret combinations in the tumultuous and war-filled forty-first year of the reign of the judges, followed by chapter II's story of Nephite modernization, another war, and Lamanite conversion. The prophecy of Nephi$_2$ takes up most of the original chapter III, after which chapter IV provides a brief poetic interlude before the book concludes, in chapter V, with the prophecy of Samuel the Lamanite. In the course of these five sketches or vignettes, Mormon hopes to show readers something new about this portion of the Nephite story. Taking our cue from Mormon's obvious editorial care, we will follow each of these chapters one by one. (For clarity, I use arabic numerals to refer to the chapter divisions in today's LDS edition of the Book of Mormon and roman numerals for the original 1830 chapter breaks.)

What, though, does this five-part structure prepare us to see? The very first words of the text offer a clue. Like the text it introduces, the heading to the book of Helaman is carefully organized and speaks to the theological concerns of the narrative. This heading divides into two parallel halves, one describing "an account of the Nephites...even down to the coming of Christ" and the other "an account of the righteousness of the Lamanites...even down to the coming of Christ." The Nephites' triple "wars and contentions, and their dissensions" is offset by another triple in the second half that reports "the righteousness of the Lamanites, and the wickedness and abominations of the Nephites." Even more striking, the heading contains only one complete sentence, and it sits dead center as the heading's organizational pivot: "And also many of the Lamanites are converted." Dividing the heading cleanly in half and serving as the only full sentence in a sea of clipped phrases, this mention of the Lamanite conversion is literally as central to the heading as it will be to the theme of the book that follows (see FIGURE 1).

## Heading to the Book of Helaman

*Part I (Nephites)*

An account of the Nephites.
Their wars, and contentions,
and their dissensions.

And also the prophecies of many holy
prophets, before the coming of Christ.

> according to the records of Helaman,
> who was the son of Helaman, and also
> according to the records of his sons,

> even down to the coming of Christ.

And also many of the Lamanites are converted.
An account of their conversion.

*Part II (Lamanites)*

An account of the righteousness of
the Lamanites, and the wickedness
and abominations of the Nephites,

> according to the record of
> Helaman and his sons,

> even down to the coming of Christ,

which is called the book
of Helaman, and so forth.

FIGURE 1  Book of Helaman heading divided into phrases

8

Before we've even begun to read a single verse, then, the heading alerts readers to keep their eyes on a comparison between Nephites and Lamanites—with the reminder, moreover, that the Nephites will not come off favorably. Whatever readers are supposed to see about the Nephite situation in the book of Helaman, it must always be projected against the Lamanites and always with an eye toward the relationship between these two branches of Lehi and Sariah's children.

It's easy to see this Nephite-Lamanite comparison reflected in the original 1830 structure of Helaman. Chapters I and II, for instance, flip back and forth between focusing narrative attention on the Nephites and on the Lamanites. These chapters are peppered, too, with comparative appraisals such as "[The Nephites] were wicked even like unto the Lamanites" (Hel. 4:22) and "[The Lamanites'] righteousness did exceed that of the Nephites" (6:1). After these first two chapters establish the comparison, the second half of the book cements it by holding up a preacher from each nation: a Nephite prophet (Nephi, chapter III) and a Lamanite prophet (Samuel, chapter V) together reaffirm that destruction awaits the Nephites, while the now-righteous Lamanites will have their days mercifully prolonged.

Just as Helaman is broadly comparative in its big-picture juxtaposition of the Nephites and the Lamanites, it is also narrowly comparative in the small-picture contrasts that organize each chapter. The original chapter I, for instance, contrasts the power-seeking methods of Nephite dissenters with the power-seeking methods of secret combinations, showing how the Nephites' blindness to the latter sets them up for their eventual destruction. As another example, chapter II contrasts the Lamanites' miraculous conversion and total repentance (Hel. 5) with the Nephites' rampant pursuit of wealth (Hel. 3) and halfway repentance in the face of military defeat (Hel. 4). In each chapter, readers are thus taught to question the accuracy of the Nephites' self-assessment and are given an illustration of the blindness that so often plagues God's people. Each original chapter contains at least one internal comparison of this sort:

Chapter I (Hel. 1–2)         *Secret combinations*
                             *and Nephite dissenters*

Chapter II (Hel. 3–6)        *Nephite wickedness and*
                             *Lamanite righteousness*

Chapter III (Hel. 7–10)      *The prophet Nephi₂ and*
                             *secret combinations*

Chapter IV (Hel. 11–12)      *Nephite wickedness*
                             *and the earth*

Chapter V (Hel. 13–16)       *The prophet Nephi₂ and*
                             *the prophet Samuel*

Though many of these parallels will become clear only in the course of our reading, it is evident that there is real care and deliberation in this book's organization. In order to understand Helaman's message, we must be sensitive to the way it presents that message to readers.

*the theme of the book of Helaman*
Finally—and most urgently, from the text's perspective—a brief word on theme. The book of Helaman would not be structured in this way unless it were trying to show us something. Comparison is a rhetorical tool used to make something visible, and, as it turns out, visibility is the name of the game in Helaman. At every turn, the text directs our attention to what is

overlooked. The Nephites court destruction, we learn, because they look in the wrong direction. Distracted by the glitter of wealth, they fail to notice secret combinations taking residence in the shadows; preoccupied with military rivalries, they grow blind to their own spiritual decadence; racially prejudiced, they misunderstand the cosmic signs of Samuel the Lamanite even when they are written across the sky in plain daylight. Virtually every character and object within the book of Helaman is related to the twin themes of visibility and invisibility. Secret combinations threaten from dark alleys, and the identity of assassins is hidden from view, all while over-the-top spectacles of money and politics distract from more pressing spiritual concerns residing invisibly in the heart. The book of Helaman is a masterclass in sight and learning to probe what goes unseen in our lives and our relationships. Had the Nephites enjoyed better eyesight, the text implies, they might have rewritten the entire Book of Mormon.

It is for this reason, in fact, that I want to make a somewhat surprising claim about the most significant verses in the book. Helaman's most important passage, to my mind, is not found in Helaman 5 with its mass Lamanite conversion or its rich teachings about Christ or even its beautiful and oft-cited description of the "rock of our Redeemer" (verse 12) but rather in an out-of-the-way place in the previous chapter: Helaman 4:20–26. This is where we watch the Nephites almost correct their sight and view themselves rightly, only to thwart self-honesty by veering toward racial rivalry instead. Though I'll say more about this passage when we come to chapter II, for now it is enough to note that we readers, as well, must keep our eyes on the subtle passages made invisible by the grooves of our usual reading. Just as the most powerful influences in our lives are the ones we can't see, the most revealing moment of Nephite blindness is tucked invisibly into the shadows cast by Helaman's more spectacular and famous chapters.

The Nephites are in deep trouble, but they can't see it. They're looking in the wrong direction, burying their heads in the sand, and laughing off every warning sign. The book of Helaman recounts a number of attempts to correct their sight, marshaling heaven and earth, military captains, chief judges, prison walls, assassins, earthquakes, cloaks and daggers, heavenly fire, Lamanite prophets, and solar movements—a whole cast of characters and set pieces who hope to show the Nephites the precarity of their spiritual situation. As those familiar with the Book of Mormon know, the Nephites don't see it. The job of the book of Helaman is to make sure that we, as readers, do.

# I

## Helaman 1 – 2

*business as usual?*

The book of Helaman opens on what looks, at first, like a scene familiar from the book of Alma: threats to the chief judgeship, dissenters stirring up Lamanite armies, and a smattering of military scuffles. Because the Nephites remain trapped in their typical cycle of political infighting and tribal conflict, and because that conflict is narrated together with a cast of characters already familiar from the second half of Alma, Helaman 1 can feel utterly routine. But there are hints that the fortieth year of the reign of the judges is far from business as usual. In truth, the Nephites are more dysfunctional than ever, and their disfunction is beginning to take unprecedented form.

The original chapter I opens with a problem among brothers: three of Pahoran$_1$'s sons (Pahoran$_2$, Paanchi, and Pacumeni) are competing for a vacancy in the chief judgeship (Hel. 1:3), and while fraternal conflict may feel utterly banal at this point in the Book of Mormon, there's at least this small hint of change in the air: for the first time, there are *three* contenders rather than two. This may seem like a small matter—after all, what's one more electoral candidate?—until we notice that nowhere else in the Book of Mormon has a succession crisis split the people three ways. When the book's first fraternal conflict arose between Nephi$_1$ and his brothers, the elder two were narrated together as a single unit (Nephi$_1$ vs. Laman-and-Lemuel), and when Lehi's death ultimately fractured the family, the family split in half rather than into thirds. In the history-heavy book of Alma as well the Nephites only ever choose between a pro-judge majority and a dissenting, monarchically nostalgic minority. Every other moment of dissent in the Book of Mormon up until this point has resulted in a two-way contest. When Helaman 1:3 alerts us that the Nephites experience a three-way split instead, readers should hear this not as a routine narration of political history but as an announcement that civic tensions are ratcheting up.

Out of this crisis comes another alarming "first" in Nephite history: the murder of a chief judge. As anticipated, the pending election produced a winner (Pahoran$_2$) and two losers (Pacumeni and Paanchi), but not every brother was content to accept this outcome. Unlike Pacumeni, who conceded the race (1:6), Paanchi planned a desperate power grab: "He was about to flatter away [his followers] to rise up in rebellion against their brethren" (verse 7), but the plot was discovered and he was "condemned unto death" (verse 8) by the newly elected government. In response to this verdict, however, and still highlighting the new extremes of political unrest among the Nephites, Paanchi's followers do something entirely unprecedented. Rather than taking up arms in public protest or defecting to the Lamanites, as Nephite dissenters so often do, they instead assassinated Pahoran$_2$ and took a protective oath of secrecy (verses 9–11). Succession disputes may be standard among the Nephites, but not when those disputes result in a three-way split or the outright murder of a legitimately elected chief judge.

Nor does the unrest end there. Just a few months later, a Lamanite army strikes another one-of-a-kind blow against the Nephites by capturing their capital city in a surprise assault (verses 18–20), requiring the general, Moronihah, not only to retake Zarahemla but even, it is hinted, to impose martial law on the city: "It came to pass that Moronihah took possession of the city of Zarahemla" and "established again peace" (verse 33; 2:1). It is in these chaotic circumstances of crumbling Nephite political infrastructure that Helaman$_2$ comes to the chief judgeship. And while Mormon is careful to describe Helaman$_2$'s election as democratically legitimate (he was, after all, "appointed...by the voice of the people" [2:2]), the text also hints at the turbulence of Helaman$_2$'s nomination. Not only was there considerable "contention... concerning who should fill the judgment-seat" (verse 1) immediately before the election, but Helaman$_2$ is targeted by another assassination attempt immediately after. The same group of dissidents responsible for the death of Pahoran$_2$ also plot against Helaman$_2$'s life (verse 3), commissioning the same assassin as before—a man named Kishkumen whose mission is foiled only by a wily servant who infiltrates their band, learns their signs and plans, and stabs Kishkumen en route to the judgment seat (verse 9). Not since the turbulent days of Lehi$_1$ and Sariah's flight from Jerusalem has the Book of Mormon reported such violent conflict among brothers coupled with murder in the streets by night (See 1 Ne. 4:7, 18).

By the end of the original chapter I, then, readers understandably crave a tidy resolution to this narrative chaos, making it all too easy to breathe a sigh of relief when Moronihah successfully retakes Zarahemla (Hel. 1:33) or Kishkumen's band retreats into the wilderness (2:11). Instead of reassuring us, however, Mormon concludes his opening chapter with a warning: "And behold, in the end of this book ye shall see...the overthrow, yea, almost the entire destruction of the people of Nephi" (verse 13). Political unrest and military conflict may feel old hat after the book of Alma, but

Mormon underlines the events of this chapter as something new. For the first time, a democratic election has collapsed into a series of assassination plots, only to be followed immediately by a foreign invasion and enemy capture of the capital. For the first time, Mormon inserts his editorial voice into the book of Helaman to mark the magnitude of Nephite dysfunction with the result that readers, also for the first time, can see the Nephites' total destruction drawing near. In short: the Nephites are slipping. Their society is splintering in more directions than ever before, leading them to new heights of political violence, and it's in this turbulent landscape that Mormon chooses to underline the existential stakes of these years for the Nephites.

But even more than emphasizing the scale of the trouble, Mormon's editorial comment also pinpoints exactly where the trouble starts: it is one "Gadianton," in particular, who "did prove the overthrow...of the people of Nephi" (2:13). Out of all the "firsts" in this opening chapter, Mormon insists, the most novel and unprecedented—and by far the most dangerous— begins with one man and his "secret combination."

*secret combinations*

The original chapter I may find the Nephites in an unprecedented level of turmoil, but that is not where Mormon shines his editorial spotlight. He focuses readers' attention on what takes place in the shadows of the fortieth year. Behind the overt political and military chaos that occupies the Nephites, a new kind of political faction quietly forms itself around Pahoran$_2$'s assassin, and so Mormon supplements his account of the Nephites' daytime civic concerns with the nighttime movements of this murderous band. While the Nephites are distracted by the assassination of their newly elected chief judge, Mormon directs readers' attention to the assassin himself; as the Nephites wrangle over who to elect in Pahoran₂'s place, Mormon keeps our eyes on the conspirators' attempts to thwart that election; and when a brash Lamanite army marches onto center stage, Mormon points his finger at the shadowy group furtively exiting the city.

The assassin in question is "one Kishkumen," who dispatched the chief judge and then bound his accomplices in a "covenant...that they would tell no man that Kishkumen had murdered Pahoran" (1:9, 11). Still reeling from this first crisis, however, the Nephites are soon distracted by a second: an army of Lamanites takes the capital city, "led by a man whose name was Coriantumr...a dissenter from among the Nephites" (verse 15). In a matter of months, then, the Nephites are hit with two devastating blows: an internally destabilized government and an externally destabilizing military threat. Though this quick succession of disasters places the Nephites in an unenviable position, Mormon nevertheless finds in it a unique teaching opportunity. Kishkumen's band and Coriantumr's army arrive together on the scene of Nephite history, both undeniable threats to the Nephites, and yet each operates by completely different methods. Indeed, the original chapter I (Hel. 1–2) deliberately compares these two groups, playing Kishkumen's secretive technology of power against Coriantumr's more familiar and overt forms of military control. By highlighting these different tactics, Mormon can also highlight the unique risks posed by secret combinations—and, more importantly, why the Nephites failed to see them.

The best way to highlight a difference, of course, is to place it against a backdrop of similarities; in order to sharpen the contrast between Coriantumr's army and Kishkumen's band, Mormon also needs to outline what they share in common. The original chapter

I thus reads like a laundry list of identical aims and results: both groups are explicitly motivated by "anger" (1:9, 16–17), both seek power (verse 16; 2:5), and both are responsible for the death of a chief judge (1:9, 21). Oddly enough, both groups are led by a man whose name carries Jaredite associations ("Kishkumen" echoes the name "Kish" and its variants found throughout the book of Ether, while "Coriantumr" was also the name of the last Jaredite king), and both groups are described as uncountable (the members of Kishkumen's band "all could not be found" [verse 12], while Coriantumr's army was "innumerable" [verse 14]). There is also an emphasis on the clothing of each group; Mormon is careful to note that the army arrives wearing "head-plates, and . . . breastplates, and . . . all manner of shields of every kind" (verse 14), while Kishkumen first arrives on the scene "in disguise" (verse 12). In arrival and aim and consequences for Nephite public life, the dissenter-led army and the secret band of assassins seem quite similar.

Against these commonalities, then, Mormon's intended distinction sticks out like a sore thumb: where dissenters behave in brazenly *visible* ways, secret combinations favor tactics that are (unsurprisingly) *secretive*. Recall that Coriantumr's soldiers marched into Zarahemla in an overt display of military power, intentionally aiming for the capital in order to create a spectacle around their victory. Remember, too, that Coriantumr is a Nephite dissenter—part of a group that, throughout the Book of Mormon, vents its frustrations with Nephite governance by turning outward, storming out of Nephite territory and allying with the Lamanites in an open show of protest. In Coriantumr's case, as well, his aims are transparent to the reader: he hopes to "go forth against all the land" (verse 22), and when his army leaves Zarahemla, it does so with an obvious trajectory ("even towards the city of Bountiful" [verse 23]). Even their clothing is evidence of their reliance on visibility, since armor can intimidate an opponent only if it is visibly displayed; the more overtly Coriantumr's army appears well-shielded, the more likely they are to strike fear in their enemies.

Secret combinations, meanwhile, do everything they can to remain out of view. Kishkumen and his coconspirators swear an oath of secrecy (verse 11), hold meetings by night (2:6), and protect their intrigues with signs (2:7). When Paanchi loses the election, his followers quietly turn inward, allying with one another and shrouding themselves in the invisibility of oaths. They "mingle themselves among the people" (1:12) and exit Zarahemla without any indication of their destination, instead fleeing "out of the land, by a secret way, into the wilderness" until "they could nowhere be found" (2:11). And rather than dressing in clothing that depends on its visibility to function, Kishkumen assumes a disguise—an outfit that aims to conceal one's true identity but succeeds in its function only if no one recognizes it *as* a disguise in the first place. Where Nephite dissenters are conspicuous, secret combinations are practically imperceptible; if Coriantumr's army is marked by its transparency, Kishkumen's band is scrupulously opaque; and while military power takes aim at external borders, the strength of secret combinations is their ability to target the inmost heart of political stability. This is emphasized even by the locations in which each group murders a chief judge: Coriantumr killed Pacumeni "against the wall" of Zarahemla (1:21), pinning him to the visible, external surface of the city, while Kishkumen killed Pahoran$_2$ "as he sat upon the judgment-seat" (verse 9), at the inmost center of Nephite political life.

This clever use of secrecy, it seems, is what makes secret combinations so disastrous for Nephite society.

Although political intrigue and desperate power grabs and even murder have been part of Nephite civic life for decades, Mormon is clear that these political sins become newly insidious once they are coupled with secret combinations. It is only *here*, for instance, that Mormon hints at the ultimate destruction of the Nephites. He didn't do so when the Nephites first split from the Lamanites (2 Ne. 5), or when Amalickiah ascended to the Lamanite throne (Alma 47), or when the king-men threw the nation into a civil war (Alma 51). Mormon emphasizes the Nephites' "overthrow" and "entire destruction" (Hel. 2:13) *only* when political unrest goes underground. Secret combinations spell disaster for the Nephites not so much because of their content but because of their form, not for their aim but for the methods they use to achieve it, not just because they combine but because they do so in secret.

This emphasis on secrecy is woven through the story of Kishkumen's band at every point in this original opening chapter—so much so, in fact, that Helaman 1–2 challenges the common Latter-day Saint conception that secret combinations are threatening primarily for their political agenda. Again, what Mormon emphasizes above all else are the *methods* and *techniques* of Kishkumen's band rather than their *content* or *aims*. Although contemporary readers often understand secret combinations to be a calculating machine bent on gaining political power, the phenomenon described in Helaman 1 looks far less shrewd and purposeful than we tend to assume. Though political power later appears as part of Gadianton's sales pitch (2:5), there is no indication, at first, that the conspirators wish to install another candidate on the judgment seat or that they themselves are seeking political office. On the contrary, they simply "saw that [Paanchi] was condemned unto death," became "angry," and then "sent forth one Kishkumen" (1:9). Mormon portrays a group of dissidents bent on venting their frustration rather than manipulating the political scene toward any specific goal. Secret combinations arrive in the Book of Mormon narrative almost accidentally, born out of excessive anger rather than any overt thirst for political power. What is most devastating about Kishkumen's group, according to Mormon, is instead its ability to avoid detection.

Kishkumen's band gains its reputation as a power-thirsty organization only when Gadianton emerges to capitalize on their already-existing clandestine network. But Gadianton, too, is characterized more by secrecy than by specific political aims. Notice how slyly he sneaks into the narrative, completely unnoticed by readers and with completely opaque intentions. He first appears in Helaman 2:4, which opens with the explanatory word "for" ("For there was one Gadianton...") despite the fact that nothing in verse 3 requires explanation or adds new information beyond what was learned in Helaman 1. Readers are told only that he was "exceedingly expert in many words" and "therefore he became the leader of the band" (verse 4). We are given nothing about his background, his earlier role in the group, or where he learned his rhetorical prowess, nor are we given direct quotations of the speech he used to secure his leadership role. We are told that "he did flatter them" (verse 5), promising to secure political favors for his followers if they would make him chief judge, but the text fails to confirm whether this is his actual intention or whether this is merely an opportunistic ploy designed to bring the band under his control.

The invisibility of Gadianton's tactics and intentions is further emphasized by the ambiguity of the pronouns in Helaman 2:11, in which—at least for a brief moment—readers cannot distinguish between Gadianton and Kishkumen: "Behold, when Gadianton had found that Kishkumen did not return, he [Gadianton] feared lest that he [Gadianton or Kishkumen?] should be destroyed; therefore he [Gadianton] caused that his [Gadianton's or Kishkumen's?] band should follow him. And they took their flight out of the land." It's impossible to tell, at this point, whether Gadianton is first or second in command, whether he is worried for himself or for Kishkumen, and whether the band belongs to him or the now-dead assassin. The inner workings of this band are so opaque that readers are unable to peel apart its leadership structure. It may even be ambiguous to the band itself, still in transition between the two men.

The only other clue Helaman 2 gives us as to Gadianton's real significance and aims comes in verse 4. His expertise and "his craft," we learn in verse 4, is "to carry on the secret work of murder and of robbery"—to "carry on," that is, not to turn this secret work to new ends or to initiate his own novel use of Kishkumen's band. Instead, Mormon views Gadianton as a threat because he *continues* a work that has already begun and that is marked first and foremost by being "secret." Gadianton is not depicted as an innovation but instead as a point of continuity. He doesn't divert or alter or improve, we are told, he simply "carr[ies] on" (verse 4). His specific plot to become chief judge, his words, his flattery—all of that is mentioned only secondarily in the following verse (verse 5). What is most pertinent, according to Mormon, is simply that Gadianton carries on the forms of secrecy. Secret combinations, we learn, are dangerous not primarily for their political corruption (heinous though that is) but for the way that corruption takes root completely unseen.

Gadianton sneaks into the story more stealthily than any other character in the original first chapter.

Even Kishkumen, it seems, is too public and too visible, too transparent to readers, and so falls prey to someone more secretive still. The real leader of this secret band creeps up on readers out of nowhere and disappears just as quickly as he arrived. As we, like the Nephites, were distracted by the political intrigue of the judgment seat, a secret combination has formed right under our noses. With Gadianton's history and intentions kept out of view and his narrative action kept to a minimum, it is hard not to suspect that he poses such a significant threat to the Nephites primarily because he is the most invisible character at work in this opening chapter. Despite the fact that his name will remain attached to this notorious group until the very end of Nephite history (see Morm. 1:18; 2:27–28), we know next to nothing about him or how he came to warrant such infamy.

Although political corruption is clearly a central part of the original chapter I, it is not what Mormon chooses to foreground. Through the contrast between secret combinations and the dissenter-led army, and with the deliberate narrative opacity surrounding Gadianton, the text foregrounds the secretive *method* of this covert band of murderers rather than their political aims. Mormon focuses on their techniques and inner workings—exactly what secret combinations had hoped to keep hidden. The original chapter I is thus, in many ways, less concerned that readers focus on this particular band of robbers and far more invested in raising broader questions about secrecy and invisibility. It is not Gadianton's band that threatens the Nephites so much as the Nephites' own blindness and their failure to be vigilant about invisible developments. Though we have much yet to learn about the specific objects of that blindness, Mormon's message is already taking shape. Keep your eyes on what is trying to sneak into the background, he seems to say. What wants to escape our attention? What are we only too happy to overlook? It's there that the real story—and the real threat—lies.

*making visible*

The problem suggested by secret combinations is not just that invisible trends among the Nephites pose the most dangerous threats but also that too much visibility elsewhere distracts attention from seeing those threats in the first place. The Nephites are understandably preoccupied with the bold and the flashy, the public political contest and the bravura of war. But by externalizing their problems in the form of military conflict and devoting their attention to the most audacious and visible aspects of civic life, they leave room for Gadianton's band to quietly organize and escape the city in secret. Visibility, in other words, cuts both ways. Making some things visible often comes at the expense of hiding others.

What takes place in secret is often far more consequential than what takes place in the open. In a tragic illustration of human nature, the Nephites model our natural eagerness to prioritize the visible over the invisible. Our lives are shaped less by what we disclose on the surface and much more by what we hide—from God, from one another, from ourselves. Too many of us overperform our love for family members on social media to compensate for our failure to call our parents or involve our siblings in our lives. We proclaim over the pulpit our devotion for our spouse or our God to compensate for failing to regularly express that devotion in our behavior at home. We guard our hemlines but forget to guard our judgmental thoughts, flaunt financial success to compensate for relational failures, and obsess over our physical appearance to hide our terror that we are unworthy of love. In short: far too many of us prioritize observable behavior and let private devotions slide. Emphasizing the public over the private, trying to manage our visible presentation just so, we become subject to Jesus's condemnation of those who, like ostentatiously decorated tombs, "indeed appear beautiful outward, but are within full...of all uncleanness" (Matt. 23:27).

Like most people, the Nephites have lived too long on the surface, distracting themselves with wealth and conflict but leaving their hearts untended. This is a problem that plagues every major character from the original chapter I. "Hearts" are referred to four times in the course of this chapter, once again serving Mormon's plea that readers focus on what is most interior and hidden. It is precisely this invisible center that is left unguarded by both Coriantumr and Kishkumen. After his successful military gambit, Coriantumr "saw that he was in possession of the city of Zarahemla, and saw that the Nephites had fled," and, bolstered by the visible symptoms of what looked initially like success, "his heart took courage" (Hel. 1:22). Kishkumen, too, is encouraged by the sight of "a sign" given to him by Helaman₂'s servant and rashly discloses "all [his] heart" (2:7–8). This matter of hearts, however, quickly turns against both characters. Coriantumr's impulsive courage ends up plunging his army into the middle of Nephite troops (1:31), while Kishkumen finds himself wounded to the exact degree of his disclosure: "When the servant of Helaman had known all the heart of Kishkumen,...he did...stab Kishkumen even to the heart" (2:8–9). Both men take stock of their situation, looking only to the most immediate indicators, and both rashly leave their hearts unexamined in the process.

But theirs are not the only hearts left defenseless in chapter I: "[The Nephites] had not kept sufficient

26

guards in the land of Zarahemla; for they had supposed that the Lamanites durst not come into the heart of their lands" (1:18). In the central territory of their nation, in their central governing family, the Nephites are so unstable that their unfortified center is quickly colonized by military threats and secret combinations. The Nephites are vulnerable at their core. And in addition to showing readers the hidden *consequences* of that vulnerability, Helaman 1–2 is also at pains to show its *cause*. There is one more invisible trend—even more deeply hidden than secret combinations—that readers must learn to see in this opening chapter. Mormon wants us to understand not only what takes root in the Nephites' hearts but also what left those hearts unstable and unguarded in the first place, not only where all the problems ended up but where they began.

We might have expected the book of Helaman to point us first to the lack of fortifications around Zarahemla or a political situation made unusually volatile after the prolonged wars of the book of Alma, but the text refuses to make either of these stories its beginning. It is no mistake that Helaman opens where it does. The original chapter I is blindingly clear about where the Nephites' problems originate: "There began to be a serious difficulty among the people of the Nephites," we are told, when "there began to be a serious contention...among the brethren, who were the sons of Pahoran" (1:1–2). The Nephites start to have problems when something goes awry among brothers. At its core, the book of Helaman is a book about brotherhood: it begins with a conflict among three siblings and ends with Samuel the Lamanite urging his Nephite "brethren" to repent (15:1). Nor is it coincidental that Helaman 2 narrates the rise of a secret fraternal order just as a fraternal division arises between Pahoran$_1$'s sons; right when their brotherhood splits, a new brotherhood forms in its place. Even the Lamanite army, led by Nephite dissenters, is a consequence of fraternal divisions from earlier in the Book of Mormon. Coriantumr represents a faction of former Nephites who defected from their ancestral home, and any military conflict between "Nephites" and "Lamanites" inevitably echoes the original conflict between Nephi$_1$ and Laman. Both locally and internationally, currently and historically, the Nephites have their fraternal relationships wrong. From the day Lehi and Sariah's family set foot in the wilderness, brothers have been at war. At the heart not only of Nephite politics but at the heart of their families as well, new schisms are forming and old schisms are coming due, and rather than healing those old wounds, the Nephites forge ahead into new ones.

This emphasis on brotherhood is yet one more instance of the text's persistent focus on invisibility. Secret combinations are just as fraternal as they are secret, and their rise condemns the Nephites for leaving their literal brotherhoods untended. Having failed to see the stakes of their familial relationships and letting those relationships languish in invisibility, the Nephites give place for a new kind of brotherhood to organize unnoticed. Secret combinations, for all their furtiveness and mystery, are still not the most hidden or invisible moment of this text (indeed, they're all too easily visible, as attested by many readers' obsession with Gadianton's band). Their secretive rise is covering a still-deeper disorder. It is the cataclysmic schism of a family—both recent (Pahoran$_1$'s) and five hundred years earlier (Lehi$_1$'s)—that sends aftershocks through the fortieth year of the reign of the judges. To focus obsessively on secret combinations, as readers tend to do, is still to miss the fact that the Gadianton robbers are merely a symptom of a much more hidden and much more devastating shortcoming in Nephite society. Keep digging down to the bedrock, the text insists; there's something deeper still.

Running underground, like the unconscious driver of Nephite civic life, are a series of hidden habits, political organizations, and familial schisms that push the Nephites toward destruction. These early indicators of the Nephites' demise are initially quite subtle. Just as ecological disaster is first visible in the slightest aberration of weather patterns or divorce can be traced back to the barest shift in a spouse's tone of voice, the entire military history of the Nephites is first foreshadowed in the squabbling among Lehi$_1$ and Sariah's sons, and Nephite civilizational collapse is augured in the three-way disagreement between Pahoran$_2$ and his brothers. Mormon practically begs us to keep our eyes on those undercurrents rather than on the flashy politics or even the gruesome murders—to focus on what's melting into the background behind all the visible conflict. Attend to what remains hidden in quiet hearts, he warns. Guard your brotherhoods lest they spiral into Satan's counterfeits. Keep your eyes on what is hardest to see, because it's what is invisible that directs the largest outcomes. The rest of Helaman trains our eyes to look in the right directions and our minds to ask the right sorts of questions about what we find there. What have we left buried and overlooked? What have we failed to see? And how do we develop the eyesight required to see the things that God would have us keep clearly in view?

# II

## Helaman 3–6

Helaman's original chapter II opens on ostensible signs for optimism—the Nephites modernize, increase their economy, expand their territory northward, and develop a shipping industry (Hel. 3:3–13)—and yet the text seems largely uninterested in these developments. Helaman 3 dispatches ten years of the most substantial modernization in Nephite history in a mostly perfunctory tone across a mere thirty-seven verses. Mormon simply blazes through these years. Whatever else readers might make of this ominous speed, it is clear that lessons drawn from this stretch of Nephite history require a breakneck pace.

Beyond its agitated tempo, Helaman 3 sounds another ominous note in its description of a "land northward...rendered desolate and without timber" due to previous inhabitants (verses 3, 5) and which the Nephites now eagerly colonize. Readers of the Book of Mormon know that "desolation" is associated primarily with the Jaredites and that the northward territory bears all the foreboding markers of cataclysmic destruction: environmental degradation (verses 5–6), heaps of bones (Omni 1:22), ruins of buildings (Mosiah 8:8), and ancient records in an unreadable language (Mosiah 8:9, 11). Just as the rise of the Gadianton robbers in chapter I hinted at the Nephites' dangerous parallel with the Jaredites (the other Book of Mormon nation torn apart by secret combinations), the original chapter II tolls the same warning through its geography. Not only are the Nephites touching on the same themes in their spiritual and civic lives, Mormon suggests, they're encroaching onto literally the same territory.

And then, in case readers missed these hints, the text gives it to us straight: "Exceedingly great pride ... had gotten into the hearts of the people ... because of their exceedingly great riches" (Hel. 3:36). "Exceeding" wealth begets "exceeding" pride, and readers are rebuked for daring to hope that shipping industries and territorial expansions could alleviate the core wickedness presently at work among the Nephites. Economic growth plays the same role in the original chapter II that the Lamanite attack played in chapter I: a glitzy distraction that risks drawing our eyes away from the seedier undercurrents of Nephite spirituality.

In this sea of rampant capital, however, Mormon sights a lone island of faith. Floating isolated in the broader Nephite economy, there is one man still observing the commandments: Helaman$_2$, the chief judge (verse 20). Beyond his generic righteousness, Helaman$_2$ also stands out in terms of his domestic relationships. While the Nephites focus their expansion on financial and territorial ends, Helaman$_2$ expands his family: "It came to pass that he had two sons ... and they began to grow up unto the Lord" (verse 21). Where the Nephites extend their geographic reach, name new territories, and build up industries, Helaman$_2$ extends his domestic sphere, names his sons, and invests in their religious instruction. Like Mormon's opening chapter, the original chapter II urges readers to compare Nephite public life with something more private, but this time the private sphere belongs to Helaman$_2$'s family, while the public glamor attaches to the Nephites' economic concerns. Helaman$_2$'s distance from the secular, money-oriented focus of the Nephites is evident, first, in his attention to a strong family legacy: both his occupation (chief judge) and his religious observance are mediated by the example of his father. As the Nephites distance themselves from their ancestral religious traditions, Helaman$_2$ keeps his feet on the humbler road cut by his father's steps. Helaman$_2$'s interest in fathers even extends to distant patriarchs: to his eldest son "he gave ... the name of Nephi, and unto the youngest, the name of Lehi" (verse 21). Helaman$_2$ is so invested in sacred history that he symbolically writes his sons into a five-hundred-year-old prophetic story. Just as his own father set down the steps in which Helaman$_2$ would "walk," his sons will be raised with the symbolic names of their ancestral fathers hanging over their lives. Clearly, the rush and haste of contemporary modernization has not distracted Helaman$_2$ from matters of covenant.

But if these are all largely external indicators of Helaman$_2$'s familial organization, the original chapter II also gives readers something more intimate: Helaman 5 contains our first substantial quotation in the book of Helaman, seven verses of Helaman$_2$'s words to his sons (verses 5–13). It's hard to overstate what a breath of fresh air this sermon is. When Mormon narrates the history of the Nephites in this period, Christ and covenants and scripture remain entirely out of view. These seem not to be publicly available—or at least not considered to be publicly relevant—among the Nephites. Only in Helaman$_2$'s home, in a teaching moment between him and his sons, do we finally see close study of previous prophecies and talk of the Messiah. At the center of Helaman$_2$'s private life, invisible to the Nephites at large, we (finally!) find Jesus.

Interestingly, however, we find Christ framed as an object of *memory*. Helaman$_2$'s sermon is narrated retroactively, as something the adult Nephi$_2$ and Lehi$_2$ "remember" (verse 5) prior to beginning their ministry.

Within that reminiscence, the Savior is then doubly memorialized as someone whom Nephi$_2$ and Lehi$_2$ are begged to "remember, remember" (verse 12), in addition to "remembering" their namesakes, the words of King Benjamin and Amulek, and the salvation on offer through the atonement (verses 6, 9–10). If this memory of a father's sermon is already chronologically out of place, why is it reserved for this particular moment in the story? And what might the persistent theme of "remembering" have to do with the book's focus on sight? On both counts, Helaman$_2$'s words to his sons seem timely. In the middle of narrating the turbulence of Nephite life and the people's rapidly changing fortunes, Mormon pauses to affirm what is solid, stable, and real: Christ. Indeed, Christ is so solid and stable that he constitutes a proper "foundation" on which to "build" (verse 12). Amid so much modernization and economic expansion, with buildings going up all around them (3:7–11), Helaman$_2$ pleads with his sons to construct something quite different. Furthermore, just as Christ's steadiness can be an antidote to current tumult, remembering can be an antidote to contemporary blindness. If you can't see your way forward, Helaman$_2$ suggests, try looking backward instead. History is full of prophets, sermons, wise advice, models of faith, clarifying examples, and personal experience. Hindsight is 20/20, and clear vision is especially crucial when one feels sightless in the present.

The original chapter II opens, then, as the story of two economies: one individualistic, the other invested in ancestral covenants; one focused on territorial expansion, the other on domestic concern and the preservation of ancestral tradition; one housing unknown political corruption while the other houses unknown messianic teachings. Where the first builds on self-interest and looks forward to the financial opportunities of the future, the other builds on "the rock of our Redeemer" (5:12) and looks backward to the faithful word of the past. The Nephites may be plagued with blindness in the book of Helaman, but here we find one model of righteous sight: cultivated between fathers and sons, jointly unconcerned by the moneyed interests of the world, "grow[ing] up unto the Lord" (3:21).

*what the nephites see*

Preoccupied with wealth and blind to both ancient covenants and impending messiahs, Nephite society quickly goes downhill. Beginning "in the church," of all places, a violent "contention" erupts (Hel. 4:1), explodes into full-blown war with the Lamanites, and results in a majority of Nephite territory falling into enemy hands (verse 5). This shock seems, at first, like exactly the kind of wake-up call the people need, because it's in this chapter that we find *the* most important passage in the book of Helaman (verses 20–26). Backed into a corner by this military disaster, the Nephites finally turn a self-critical eye on their own situation. Indeed, one of Mormon's biggest lessons for contemporary readers turns on what the Nephites manage to "see" in these verses.

Unlike previous military straits, the Nephites' situation in Helaman 4 is unique because they find themselves at a complete standstill. Moronihah orchestrates a comeback and regains half of the Nephites' land— but *only* half. Try as they might, the Nephite army can't gain an inch more and are forced simply to maintain their meager returns (verses 9–10, 16–19). They are at such a standstill, in fact, that the text describes the two armies as perfectly matched: each possesses a clean "half" of the available territory (verse 16) and is equaled in strength "even man for man" (verse 26). Mirroring the Lamanites in muscle and territorial gains, the Nephites are stuck in gridlock, unable to do anything other than stand still and face up to the situation.

Acknowledging that their wickedness might be to blame for their current situation, the Nephites begin to concede a whole litany of wrongdoing. Notably, these sights are listed almost universally in the past perfect tense: "They saw that they *had been* a stiffnecked people, and that they *had set* at naught the commandments of God; and that they *had altered* and trampled under their feet the laws...and they saw that their laws *had become* corrupted, and that they *had become* a wicked people" (verses 21–22; emphasis added). But then, all of a sudden, something halts the flow of past examination, shocking the people back into the present. Now, instead of the past perfect tense, Mormon begins to use the simple past to indicate that, although the events narrated remain in the past for *us readers*, he is describing something that was experienced by the Nephites in their present. Even more curiously, the thing that motivates this grammatical shift seems to be the Lamanites: the Nephites suddenly realize "that they *were* wicked even like unto the Lamanites" (verse 22; emphasis added). Nor is this pattern a one-time occurrence; it continues with striking regularity in the following verses—the Nephites consistently narrate their wickedness in the past while also listing comparisons with the Lamanites in their present. In verse 24 the Nephites "saw that they *had become* weak," but as soon as they make the comparison with "their brethren, the Lamanites," the consequence is given in the present ("that the Spirit of the Lord *did* no more preserve them") (verse 24; emphasis added). In verse 25 as well the Nephites are aware that "they *had fallen* into a state of unbelief and awful wickedness," but what they see in the present is "that the Lamanites *were* exceedingly more numerous than they" (verse 25; emphasis added). Although forced into self-examination, and although presented with the opportunity to see their past more clearly, the Nephites keep returning to their present in order to compare themselves with the Lamanites.

Readers might well be suspicious of how persistently the Lamanites come to play in the Nephites' self-reflection. What do the Lamanites have to do with Nephite wickedness, after all? Secret combinations and obsessions with wealth are narrated as uniquely *Nephite* problems. Indeed, Helaman 5 is about to report just how quick to repent and how receptive to preaching the Lamanites actually are. It's hard not to suspect, in other words, that there's something shady about the way that a moment of near-repentance for the Nephites veers so sharply toward a depiction of their most hated enemies as "weak" and "wicked." Rather than seeing in simple terms how weak they are themselves, the Nephites seem willing to admit their weakness only if it comes paired with an opportunity to denigrate their adversaries. They will admit their wickedness, in other words, only if it includes a chance to scapegoat the presumed wickedness of their brothers.

The suspicious persistence of this Lamanite comparison is only the first of several hints that something is amiss in the Nephites' self-reflection. A second indication: their self-critique fails to produce any concrete results. This flash of introspection doesn't cash out in humility or repentance, a resolution to the military standstill, a new rash of converts to the church, or any other indicator of change. On the contrary, Helaman 4 closes on a conspicuous silence. Mormon simply concludes their self-reflection by noting that the Nephites had "fallen into this great transgression...in the space of not many years" (verse 26). Nor is it any mistake that the Lamanites' characterization as "wicked" and "weak" in Helaman 4:20–26 is followed immediately by the story of their conversion (Hel. 5). By failing to mention any signs of Nephite repentance and instead following their self-reflection with an overwhelming example of Lamanite humility, the text punctures the Nephites' self-congratulatory assessment of Lamanite depravity.

Twisting the screw further still, Helaman 4:20–26 is peppered with editorial additions that correct and expand the scope of Nephite self-evaluation. When the Nephites saw "that they had altered and trampled under their feet the laws of Mosiah," Mormon feels it incumbent to clarify that the laws are "that which the Lord commanded [Mosiah] to give unto the people" (verse 22). While the Nephites are distracted by their shared wickedness with the Lamanites (verse 22), he takes the opportunity to give readers a view of the consequences: "And because of their iniquity the church had begun to dwindle" (verse 23). And when the Nephites "saw . . . that the Spirit of the Lord did no more preserve them" in battle, Mormon slips in a moral lesson for readers: "Yea, it had withdrawn from them because the Spirit of the Lord doth not dwell in unholy temples" (verse 24). If we remove these additions from the passage, all that remains is a handful of limited self-assessments that immediately fuel hateful Lamanite tropes. Everything that initially seemed redemptive and encouraging and self-critical about Helaman 4:20–26 shows signs of being a narratorial addition. It's *Mormon*, not the Nephites themselves, who turns out to have the clearest eyesight in this passage, and so it's *Mormon* who supplements Nephite self-assessment with the reality of their situation.

But there is one more addition that reveals just how blinded the Nephites have become by their rivalry with the Lamanites. Tucked away at the heart of Helaman 4:20–26 is a damning reminder of the sightlessness under which the Nephites are laboring. At the very center of the passage, structurally framed as much as it is thematically emphasized, lies the *real* sight the Nephites have overlooked (see FIGURE 2):

A     "it became impossible for the Nephites to obtain more power over them" (Hel. 4:19)

B     "the greatness of the number of the Lamanites" (Hel. 4:20)

C     (quotation of an external source: Alma and Mosiah) (Hel. 4:21)

D     "they were wicked even like unto the Lamanites" (Hel. 4:22)

E     "the judgments of God did stare them in the face" (Hel. 4:23)

D     "they had become weak, like unto their brethren, the Lamanites" (Hel. 4:24)

C     (quotation of an external source: King Benjamin; see Mosiah 1:13) (Hel. 4:24–25)

B     "the Lamanites were exceedingly more numerous than they" (Hel. 4:25)

A     "the strength of the Lamanites was as great as their strength" (Hel. 4:26)

FIGURE 2   Helaman 4:20–26 structurally and thematically framed.

The Nephites are not the only ones with eyes in this scenario. God also has a perspective on their predicament, and though his judgments are staring back at them, all the Nephites seem to see is the wickedness of their enemies. The Nephites have fixated on the wrong sight. Thinking that they're looking at the Lamanites, they, in fact, see only their own *prejudices about* the Lamanites. Thinking they have a window onto their enemies, they, in fact, have just been given a mirror. What's more, by convincing themselves that they're surveying the situation objectively, they overlook the divine eye regarding them in turn.

Just as the original chapter I (Hel. 1–2) was marked by the Nephites' failure to see fraternal disorder because of their focus on a Lamanite army, the original chapter II (Hel. 3–6) is marked by their failure to see the judgments of God because of their focus on a prejudiced fantasy of Lamanite degeneracy. Both distractions are ways of letting themselves off the hook, focusing on external motes in order to avoid wrestling with personal beams. And if the unnerving "stare" of God's judgments was not enough to send a chill down readers' spines, the abrupt ending of the chapter should raise our hackles. The Nephites show no signs of repenting and, despite claims that the Nephites "saw" their predicament somewhat more clearly, Helaman$_2$'s eldest son feels the need to jettison his political career in exchange for religious ministry (5:1). The Nephites cannot repent if they cannot see clearly, and they cannot see clearly if they refuse the possibility that their perspective might be faulty. Mormon sums it up for us with devastating simplicity: "And thus had they fallen" (4:26).

*correcting vision(s)*
At the very moment the Nephites reach unprecedented extremes of hardness, however, readers are privy to

41

what is arguably the most spectacular moment of conversion in the entire Book of Mormon. Nephi$_2$ and Lehi$_2$ undertake a mission into Lamanite territory where, at first, they receive a less-than-warm welcome. Though they are initially "cast into prison" (5:21), they are held captive in a place that becomes something closer to a temple than a jail. On the very day planned for their execution, Nephi$_2$ and Lehi$_2$ are subject instead to a heavenly vision. When guards enter the prison, they find their hostages "encircled about with a pillar of fire" (verse 24), see the prison fill with smoke (verse 28), hear a divine voice (verse 29), and pray until they, too, are party to miraculous fire and angelic ministrations (verses 43, 48). Once converted, these guards spread the news of their prison Pentecost among the Lamanites until "the more part...were convinced" (verse 50) and in fact "did yield up unto the Nephites the lands of their possession" (verse 52). This Lamanite conversion, Mormon eagerly points out, ends the military standstill far more comprehensively and peacefully than ever could have been accomplished by the sword.

Even more meaningful than the miraculous fire or the divine voice or angels descending from heaven, however, is the way this conversion fulfills the hope of every Nephite prophet since the beginning of the Book of Mormon. Converting the Lamanites has been the highest wish of Book of Mormon authors since the days of Jacob (Jacob 7:24; Enos 1:11–13). Lamanite repentance is not only an answer to father Lehi's final prayer (2 Ne. 1:23, 28) but also the mission of the record his children would ultimately produce. Nor is any of this significance lost on our narrator. Helaman 5 is a textual catalog of the centuries of Nephite prophecy it fulfills. The chapter is overrun with a staggering number of parallels to earlier texts. We find shaking prisons (see Alma 14), abandoned judgment seats (see Alma

4:20), luminous prophets (see Mosiah 13), miraculous fire and angelic ministrations (see 3 Ne. 11). We hear echoes of dramatic phrases that appear only in one other place in the Book of Mormon, such as a "pillar of fire" that recalls Lehi's first vision (1 Ne. 1:6; Hel. 5:24), the Lamanites being "struck dumb with amazement" just as Korihor was famously rendered mute (Alma 30:49–50; Hel. 5:25), and a heavenly voice commanding its listeners to "seek no more to destroy" Nephi$_2$ and Lehi$_2$—the same words issued by an angel to Alma$_2$ (Alma 36:9, 11; Hel. 5:29). And if these narrative and verbal parallels were somehow not enough to mark the chapter's insistence on citing the entire Nephite tradition, Helaman 5 also includes an astonishing cast of characters mentioned directly by name, including King Benjamin (verse 9), Amulek (verse 10), Zeezrom (verse 10), Ammon (verse 21), and Limhi (verse 21), not to mention the namesakes of Lehi$_1$ and Nephi$_1$. From narrative parallels to verbal echoes to explicitly named characters, Helaman 5 is easily the most hypersaturated intertextual chapter in the entire Book of Mormon.

There is one series of parallels, however, that stands out from the rest. Though the entire Book of Mormon yearns for the repentance of the Lamanites, there is no character who represents that hope more strongly than father Lehi and no prophetic moment that voices that longing more poignantly than his tree of life vision. This was the vision, after all, introduced by Lehi's "exceeding" "fear" for his eldest sons (1 Ne. 8:4), containing the scene of Laman and Lemuel's refusal to join their family at the tree of life (verses 17–18) and concluded by Lehi's anxiety that Laman and Lemuel "should be cast off from the presence of the Lord" (verse 36). Because the events of Helaman 5 fulfill Lehi's hope for the reconciliation and joint righteousness of his sons, the chapter is also narrated as a fulfillment of his famous dream—except that this time his wayward sons make it to the tree.

First, of course, it must be noted that the two Nephite prophets who occasion this prison conversion are named after the only two Book of Mormon characters that we know of who saw the tree of life vision. Many of the set pieces are also the same: a man-made building on the verge of collapse (Hel. 5:27; 1 Ne. 11:36), a dark fog (Hel. 5:28; 1 Ne. 8:23), and a group of characters "cast[ing] their eyes about" (Hel. 5:43; 1 Ne. 8:25). Even the "pillar of fire" that envelops Nephi$_2$ and Lehi$_2$ in the prison (Hel. 5:24) has its echo in the tree of life— another white and fiery structure (see 1 Ne. 8:11) whose attainment "filled" its recipients with unspeakable "joy" (Hel. 5:44; 1 Ne. 8:12). The crucial difference between 1 Nephi 8 and Helaman 5 is simply the placement of the Lamanites. While Lehi$_1$'s original vision was tainted by the sting of Laman and Lemuel's rejection of the fruit, a happier version occurs some five hundred years later when their descendants gather at the root of the tree, beckoned through history (a history, remember, that is exhaustively cataloged by Hel. 5) by characters named Nephi$_2$ and Lehi$_2$. Sad stories can have happy endings, we learn. Old dreams ending in domestic tragedy are still available for joyful conclusions, and history is not resigned simply to citation but is also available for miraculous revision. The whole world is ripe for God to break in at any moment because lives and texts and histories are not rigid and they are not fixed—even after five hundred years of evidence to the contrary.

And if Helaman 5 mostly has its eye on those larger historical patterns, readers shouldn't miss the subtle critique it also issues against the Nephites. The events of this prison conversion not only rewrite Lehi$_1$'s vision from 1 Nephi 8 but also correct the Nephites' vision from Helaman 4:20–26. Here again, a series of parallels is instructive: like the Nephites just a chapter earlier, the Lamanites are afraid (5:23), immobilized (verse 25), and blind (verse 28). Overshadowed by a "cloud of darkness" that impedes their vision, frozen by an unexpected scene and an earthquake, the characters in the prison are at a standstill, forced into a motionless face-off where they can do little more than look around. Where the Nephites were metaphorically immobilized and blinded by their military gridlock, the Lamanites experience the same conditions literally just a few verses later.

It is in this light that we might read one of the most curious features of Helaman 5: despite Mormon's clear commitment to the literal reality of the Lamanites' experience, he nevertheless describes their prison conversion in metaphorical terms. Beginning with verse 23, the chapter marks most of these miraculous scenes with the phrase "as if:" "encircled about *as if* by fire," "*as if* they were struck dumb," "*as if* they were about to tumble," (verses 23, 25, 27; emphasis added. See also verses 29–31, 33, 36, 44–46, and 48). Over and over, the text pushes back against its own literal intent. Despite narrating a public, communal event that resists the metaphorical conventions of more psychological conversion experiences (e.g., Alma 36), Helaman 5 contains more instances of "as if" than any other chapter of Latter-day Saint scripture—by a long shot. If readers are not meant to wager a psychological reading of the Lamanite conversion, why does the text insist on marking each of these experiences in metaphorical language? And what light, in the end, will this shed on the Nephites' attitudes as portrayed in Helaman 4:20–26?

Let's begin with the expression "as if" itself. "As if" is a conjunction—it compares two words or phrases (in this case, things like "encircled about" and "fire"

[5:23]) while nonetheless implying that the comparison may not be literal. We might say that it describes a hypothetical or imaginary situation that, despite being unreal, impacts the current situation in some way. For instance, imagine that I said my friend was "acting as if he were the king of England." Despite being factually inaccurate, picturing my friend as English royalty helps to clarify something about his pompous behavior. But "as if" is not simply an indication that a comparison is false. It can also be used to acknowledge one's uncertainty, such as when I remark that "it sounds as if you're coming down with a cold." In both cases, "as if" marks a description as hypothetical at the same time that it draws on that hypothetical situation in order to clarify a present situation.

By marking the text with such a concentrated rash of "as ifs," Helaman 5 functions more like noting someone's pending cold than it does like comparing my friend to a British monarch. Rather than implying that these events didn't happen, Helaman 5 intends to say something about the Lamanites' perspective. Every "as if" in this chapter draws our attention to the appearance *as an appearance*, functioning less as an expression of doubt and more as a way to render these sights emphatically visual. If Nephi$_2$ and Lehi$_2$ were merely "encircled about with fire," for instance, there would be less emphasis on the spectacle and more emphasis on its narrative impact. When the text reports, however, that they were "encircled about *as if* with fire," it draws our attention to the fact that there's an image on display awaiting evaluation and calls us to examine our relation to it. In this way, readers are invited to grapple with these events as *perceptions* before digesting them as straightforward narrative data—forced, that is, to take them in as *sights* rather than happenings that immediately give way to the next event in the flow of the story. It *looked like* fire, it *seemed* like the prison might fall, the voice *appeared* to be above the cloud. The point is not to doubt that any of these appearances were real but rather to emphasize that they are nonetheless first presented to the Lamanites as appearances. We are not meant to focus on the Lamanites' brains, trying to discern how much doubt those brains did or did not contain; readers are meant, rather, to pay attention to the Lamanites' *eyes*.

What's more, by marking those eyes under the hesitation of the phrase "as if," Helaman 5 portrays the Lamanites' perspective as careful, self-critical, and cautious about appearances—everything the Nephites failed to be in Helaman 4:20–26. Refusing both hasty insistence on the reality of these spectacles and a reactionary psychologism that would portray the Lamanites as implicitly doubting, Helaman 5 uses the phrase "as if" to demonstrate the gap between appearance and reality and to associate the Lamanites with an admirable awareness of that gap. Cognizant that there might be more here than meets the eye, but without therefore becoming rational skeptics, the Lamanites seek more information.

Note, for instance, that the Lamanites "durst not lay their hands upon [Nephi$_2$ and Lehi$_2$] for fear lest they should be burned" (verse 23). Far from archly intoning skepticism about whether or not there was *actual* fire, the Lamanites believe in the appearance enough to feel its heat. They act in accordance with their sight at the same time that the narrative exhibits care about its literalness. Because they are sensitive to what their eyes tell them but nonetheless careful about the limitations of their perspective, the Lamanites are able to see precisely what the Nephites had overlooked just a few verses before: "Behold, it is God that has shown unto you this marvelous thing" (verse 26). Like the Nephites, the Lamanites are here shown that they "cannot...slay" their opponents (verse 26), but unlike the Nephites, the Lamanites also prove able to see the hand of God behind it.

Once we notice that sight and visibility structure this conversion experience, other features begin to stand out. The first is that Nephi$_2$ and Lehi$_2$ play a mostly silent, passive role in the Lamanites' instruction. They may glow like Abinadi or inhabit a quaking prison like Alma$_2$ and Amulek, but they issue no instructions or sermons like their prophetic predecessors. Rather than adding veracity to their words, their shining faces instead seem purely pragmatic: they render Nephi$_2$ and Lehi$_2$ visible through the cloud of darkness. Indeed, the turning point of the whole story begins with a literal pivot by a Nephite dissenter who is able to see Nephi$_2$ and Lehi$_2$'s glowing faces through the haze (verse 36). Notice, too, that when this dissenter (named Aminadab, we later learn [verse 39]) finally redirects his gaze to the two Nephite prophets, he sees them looking elsewhere. It is not their words that direct him toward God but their eyes. Nephi$_2$ and Lehi$_2$ are not simply speaking to "some being" but specifically "to some being *whom they beheld*" (verse 36; emphasis added). The Lamanites are converted not only by holding a suspensive, careful relationship to their own sight but also by perceiving that there is something they haven't seen. Gazing on others gazing elsewhere, the Lamanites realize that they are missing something crucial.

It's also telling that the Lamanites' first words in this scene are questions rather than declarative statements. Careful not to rush to conclusions but also unashamed to reveal their ignorance, the Lamanites immediately look for more information. Notice, too, that they don't inquire about the spectacle immediately before them. Rather than asking by what power Nephi$_2$ and Lehi$_2$ avoid being burned, or why their faces are shining, or how to evade destruction, they first ask how to *interpret* what they see ("what do all these things mean") and then to *identify* the invisible being implied by Nephi$_2$ and Lehi$_2$'s gaze ("and who is it with whom these men do converse?" [verse 38]). Their questions are interpretive (verse 38) before they are pragmatic (verse 40). Rather than being drawn like moths to the flame of the flashy display in the prison, the Lamanites seem to realize that what they see are merely symptoms of something deeper and more urgent.

Prompted, then, by Aminadab's instruction to "repent, and cry unto the voice, even until ye shall have faith in Christ" (verse 41), the Lamanites get to work relating to this invisible God. Instead of orienting themselves to the signs of God's presence, they orient themselves to God himself. Rather than trying to put out the fire, they begin to examine their personal sins. Rather than figuring out how to escape a structurally unstable building, they commit themselves to their knees. Rather than deriving an encyclopedia of propositional information about the Nephite deity, they learn on the fly how to worship his Son. They do not want simply to learn *about* the invisible register that organizes their situation but to fit themselves to it. The result? "The cloud of darkness was dispersed from overshadowing them," and "behold, they...were encircled about, yea every soul, by a pillar of fire" (verse 43). This time the fire is not described in metaphorical terms. Perhaps because the fire is no longer a spectacle, the "as if" drops away. Because the Lamanites have joined Nephi$_2$ and Lehi$_2$ in a worshipful posture relative to heaven, their experience of the fire is now a proper *experience* rather than a sight.

Mormon's original chapter II (Hel. 3–6) encourages its readers to behave like these Lamanites. The text celebrates the Lamanites for holding their interpretations lightly and critiques the Nephites for failing to do so. As a result of this failure, the Nephites overlook the redemptive possibilities God held in store: five centuries of covenant hope were unexpectedly fulfilled overnight in a small prison in the land of Nephi, and an entire war was ended by the actions of two mostly passive preachers (5:51–52). Think how differently Helaman 4:20–26 would read—how much more accurately and charitably—if the Nephites had viewed their situation "*as if* like unto the Lamanites," if they'd expressed even minor hesitation about a prejudicial assessment of their enemies. Mormon issues a corrective of Nephite blindness through the Lamanites' model of rightly ordered sight. By holding their interpretations lightly, taking care with the data they receive from their eyes, and staying alert to the invisible forces at work in their lives, the Lamanites prove capable of seeing God.

*the return of the gadiantons*

As soon as Mormon turns his editorial attention back to the Nephites, however, a predictable scene comes into view: "The Nephites . . . had become hardened and impenitent and grossly wicked" (Hel. 6:2). After a brief calm motivated only by the Nephites' economic gain (verses 7–14), readers are sharply reminded of just how little has really changed: "In the sixty and sixth year . . . behold, Cezoram was murdered by an unknown hand as he sat upon the judgment-seat" (verse 15). We're right back where we began, with unknown hands assassinating chief judges while the Nephites "set their hearts upon their riches" (verse 17). Despite all the intervening prophecy and preaching and dramatic Lamanite conversion that has occurred since Helaman 1, the Nephites haven't budged an inch.

Hoping to demonstrate how completely the situation after the Lamanites' conversion blindly mirrors the

A    Economic growth
     (Hel. 3:3–12)

B    Moronihah, Nephi$_2$, and Lehi$_2$ preach
     to the Nephites (Hel. 4:14–17)

C        Territorial consequences + Nephites compared
         with Lamanite *wickedness* (Hel. 4:18–26)

D            Lamanite conversion
             (Hel. 5)

C        Territorial consequences + Nephites compared
         with Lamanite *righteousness* (Hel. 5:50–6:1)

B    Lamanites, Nephi$_2$, and Lehi$_2$ preach
     to the Nephites (Hel. 6:4–6)

A    Economic growth
     (Hel. 6:7–14)

FIGURE 3 Comparison of Lamanites before and after conversion.

situation before, all of the original chapter II is organized as one enormous series of parallels (see FIGURE 3).
    In fact, the only two phenomena of Nephite his-
tory not captured by these parallels are a brief period
of growth among the church (which was quickly under-
mined; see 3:24–26, 33) and the return of the Gadianton
robbers, which occupies most of Helaman 6. If this structure reflects the sorts of interests that most occupy the
Nephites—things like wealth and their relationship with
the Lamanites—Helaman 6 shows readers what is once
again left out of their view: secret combinations. Still too
focused on the breach with the Lamanites (whether still
persisting or recently overcome), the Nephites in chapter

II remain as blind to Gadianton's band as they were when it first formed in chapter I. Secret combinations creep up among the Lamanites as well, but once again readers have reason to be impressed with the Lamanites' eyesight. The Lamanites "did hunt the band" until it was "utterly destroyed from among [them]" (6:37). Among the Nephites, however, secret combinations don't even rise to visibility: "Behold, they were not found" (verse 19).

The point of Mormon's original chapter II, then, is not only to report on a miraculous conversion among the Lamanites but also to show how little impact that conversion had among the Nephites. Chapter II systematically undermines any optimism readers might have felt upon reading the events of Helaman 5, forcing us to feel the despair that should attend any reading of Nephite fate and that Mormon, as one of the last Nephites standing, felt so acutely. Helaman 5 may have represented the culmination of the Nephite prophetic tradition, but that only makes it all the more devastating when the covenant is forsaken by the Nephites in the chapters on either side. Laman and Lemuel have symbolically joined the rest of the family at the tree of life only to watch in disbelief as $Nephi_1$ heads off to the great and spacious building.

The original chapter II thus warns readers against falling into the same trap as the Nephites. Just as the people are easily distracted by the glitter of gold and the shouts of impending Lamanite armies, readers are easily distracted by the bright lights and loud noises of the conversion narrative in Helaman 5, as well as (understandably) the devotion and hopefulness it inspires. That's all well and good, suggests Mormon, but don't lose sight of what threatens its effectiveness. Worshipful devotion is only as useful as our ability to sustain it. We must focus on what goes unseen, Mormon teaches, because our lives are controlled by what is most invisible to us.

This does not mean, of course, that we must fret about what political opponents might be doing behind closed doors or that we must become rational skeptics, using the logic of "as if" to insulate ourselves from reality and render ourselves intellectually sovereign. If chapter I taught us to keep our eyes on what escapes notice, chapter II identifies what always goes most unnoticed of all: ourselves. Our assumptions, our prejudices, our biases, and our fears are all more immediate spiritual threats than anything at work in the world around us. It's for this reason that, although chapter II centers on one of the richest conversions in the Book of Mormon, we mustn't miss how it closes: "Thus we see that [the Nephites] were in an awful state, and ripening for an everlasting destruction" (6:40).

# III

## Helaman 7–10

Nephi$_2$, the son of Helaman$_2$, has been gone from Zarahemla for roughly six years, preaching a mission with his brother (Hel. 7:2). Unlike the original chapter II, which covered twenty-five years and several crucial episodes, the original chapter III centers on a single story that unfolds over just two days immediately upon Nephi$_2$'s return. This story moves *fast*—so fast, in fact, that Mormon gives us virtually no information about its main character. We don't read about Nephi$_2$'s spiritual development, his time as a chief judge, or any of the public speeches he presumably gave as such a prominent political and religious leader. Even in Helaman 5, Nephi$_2$ was mostly peripheral to the Lamanites' conversion. Though it isn't clear why Mormon keeps Nephi$_2$ on the sidelines prior to this point, this low visibility makes for a dramatic scene when Nephi$_2$ returns to Zarahemla.

Setting foot in his home city for the first time in six years, Nephi$_2$ is completely overcome by the degree of moral depravity and political corruption he finds there. Though his time in the land northward was not particularly encouraging (7:3), it's another matter entirely to discover that Nephite decadence extends all the way to the heart of the nation. In comparison to his inspiring successes among the Lamanites, the situation of the Nephites must strike an acute blow. Horrified by the sight of what his people have become in "the space of not many years," Nephi$_2$ "bowed himself upon the tower which was in his garden" and began to "exclaim in the agony of his soul" (verses 6, 10).

Whether by calculation or by chance, Nephi$_2$'s lament draws a crowd. Noticing the growing group of onlookers, Nephi$_2$ voices one of the now-familiar themes of the book of Helaman: the Nephites can see him and his emotion, but can they see *themselves*? "Because of my mourning and lamentation ye have gathered yourselves together, and do marvel," he warns, but "ye ought to marvel because ye are given away that the devil has got so great hold upon your hearts" (verse 15). The devil's vise grip on the people, Nephi$_2$ goes on to say, stems from two primary sins: they "have set [their] hearts upon the riches...of this world," leading them to "murder, and plunder, and steal" (verse 21). Or, in other words: "Wo be unto you because of that great abomination which has come among you...that secret band which was established by Gadianton," and "Wo...because of your exceedingly great riches!" (verses 25–26). The two problems that characterize the Nephites, each doubly emphasized, are (1) wealth and (2) secret combinations. Nephi$_2$ can see in a single glance what the Nephites have overlooked about themselves for nearly three decades.

Nephi$_2$'s strong emotion provokes an equally emotional response from Gadianton-affiliated judges in the crowd, who attempt to rile the audience into dragging Nephi$_2$ to court (8:1–2). Some in the crowd nevertheless defend him, and, seeing that he's starting to gain some traction (verses 7–9), Nephi$_2$ legitimates his predictions of destruction with scriptural precedent. God granted power to ancient prophets, he reasons, so why should the people doubt that God might grant to Nephi$_2$, as well, power to recognize their sin? (verses 11–12). Even more importantly, he uses this mention of prophets to turn the people's attention to the coming Messiah (verses 13–23). The pressing imminence of Nephite wickedness, however, forces Nephi$_2$ to prioritize his oracle of destruction over the Jesus-centered message he only started to give. Helaman 8 concludes instead with Nephi$_2$'s dramatic real-time announcement of the chief judge's murder ("Behold, your judge is murdered"; verse 27), setting in motion a series of narrative events that carry Nephi$_2$ far beyond the doctrinal message of redemption he might have preferred.

On his tower and in the subsequent court scene, Nephi$_2$ finds himself in a tricky situation. He needs both to call the people to repentance for enabling the rise of secret combinations and to elude the governmental authority of the Gadianton operatives standing in the very crowd in front of him. Furthermore, directing attention to secret combinations is difficult in its own right: How can you point your finger at something that prides itself on its invisibility? Nephi$_2$'s solution is brilliant. Beginning in Helaman 8, Nephi$_2$ *himself* performs the tactics of secret combinations. Because he can't point at something invisible, he mirrors their methods; because he can't make the Gadiantons own up to their schemes, *Nephi$_2$* impersonates them instead.

For instance, notice that his prophecy of a coming Messiah is framed as secret knowledge held by a prophetic brotherhood: "Behold I say unto you, that Abraham not only knew of these things, but there were many before the days of Abraham who were called by the order of God . . . that it should be shown unto the people . . . that even redemption should come unto them" (verse 18). Abraham and his predecessors are described as a fraternal "order" oriented around a piece of information that is not public knowledge, ironically parroting the way secret combinations organize their depraved brotherhood around similarly secret information. Likewise, Nephi$_2$ reports that the Nephites' pending destruction has been "made...known" to him by God (7:29), echoing Kishkumen's disclosure of murderous plans to Helaman's servant—the only earlier instance of the phrase "made known" in the book of Helaman (2:7). And, like all secret combination operatives, Nephi$_2$ verifies his fraternal knowledge with a sign (i.e., the murder of the chief judge), just as the servant gave "a sign" to Kishkumen as evidence that he was trustworthy (see 2:7). By echoing secret combination tactics in this ironic reversal, Nephi$_2$ drags their methods into daylight so they can be seen more clearly.

Nephi$_2$'s mirroring grows only more intense as the scene proceeds. His announcement—"Your judge is murdered, and he lieth in his blood; and he hath been murdered by his brother" (8:27)—is a crucial turning point in the story. It sets off a secondary scene in Helaman 9 where, after an interlude of misunderstandings, the judges assume that Nephi$_2$ was in on the murder and so he delivers a second sign to verify the first. Taken together, Nephi$_2$'s two signs (the first sign announcing the chief judge's murder and the second sign identifying his killer) continue to echo the techniques of secret combinations. For one thing, Nephi$_2$'s signs expose the very information that secret combinations were initially formed to hide: the identity of a chief judge's assassin (1:11). Additionally, although the Gadiantons pride themselves on insulating any of their members from being "injured by his brother" (6:22), the chief judge has here been murdered by his brother quite literally (8:27)!

As the scene progresses, Nephi$_2$ also begins to mirror the kind of detailed scripting required by Gadianton operatives. Charging his audience to confront the murderer, he explains, "Ye shall say unto him: Have ye murdered your brother? And he shall stand with fear, and wist not what to say. . . . And ye shall find blood upon the skirts of his cloak. And when ye have seen this, ye shall say: . . . Do we not know that it is the blood of your brother? And then shall he tremble, and shall look pale, even as if death had come upon him" (9:29–33). Though readers usually see this predictive accuracy as proof of Nephi₂'s prophetic commission, we should note that it also parrots the kind of foresight required for political manipulation—an uncanny insight into an opponent's thoughts, behaviors, and likely responses. To the Gadianton robbers in attendance, Nephi₂ looks like the consummate strategist. It is likely for this reason that the judges assume he has arrived at this knowledge through conspiracy (verse 16). Because Nephi₂ has mirrored their fraternal logic, use of signs, and political scripting, they assume he must be playing their game in its entirety, right down to committing murder in order to secure power. Nephi₂ has so effectively mirrored the logic of the Gadianton robbers that they suspect him of representing a rival secret combination himself.

Nephi₂ thus forces the judges and the people at large into the same self-reflexive visibility that the Nephites had begun to confront in Helaman 4:20–26. By emulating their conspiratorial tactics in plain daylight, Nephi₂ forces the Gadianton operatives to face themselves. But Nephi₂ is also attempting to force visibility on the people as a whole. Announcing the chief judge's murder is just as much about alerting them to the imminence of their destruction—that it "is now even at your doors," as he says (8:27)—as it is about verifying Nephi₂'s prophetic power. The sign reveals just how far the Gadiantons have infiltrated Nephite government, signals that something is once again awry among brothers, and serves as an avatar of the violent end that meets the wicked. Prophets *should* be able to spend their time preaching about the Messiah, but instead Nephi$_2$ is forced to point out what is already painfully obvious.

Even more than securing Nephi$_2$'s prophetic authority, in other words, this announcement of the chief judge's death illustrates the fate that awaits the people: brother turned against brother, knives at the ready. Indeed, Nephi$_2$'s second sign with its description of the murderer can be read as an especially clear reflection of the Nephites' precarity. Like the assassin, the people may be alive and breathing and secure in the belief that their wickedness is invisible, but it will not last long. Soon they, too, will come to resemble their chief judge. Indeed, in several important ways, the chief judge's brother is described in terms that resemble the very man he has just killed: "Behold, ye shall examine him, and ye shall find blood upon the skirts of his cloak.... And then shall he tremble, and shall look pale, even as if death had come upon him" (9:31, 33). Like his victim, the murderer is found with blood on his clothing, trembling in the final throes of life as his fate is sealed, the blood draining out of his face until he physically resembles a cadaver. Though living and breathing, this man is little more than a pre-corpse, at this point. On his way to being condemned for assassination, he is an avatar of the Nephites who think they're getting away with murder all the while having one foot in the grave. Though the Nephites are convinced of their own power and autonomy, under Nephi$_2$'s gaze they become little more than characters in a pathetically transparent script.

The problem, of course, is that the Nephites refuse to see. Despite the accuracy of Nephi$_2$'s assessment, the clarity of his call to repentance, and the disturbing vividness of the consequences that await them, the Nephites exchange the invisible implications of Nephi$_2$'s sermon for the spectacle of Nephi$_2$ himself. Nephi$_2$ had hoped that his signs might give credibility to his testimony of Christ, just as Jeremiah's prediction of the destruction of Jerusalem and Moses's power to heal Israel earned credibility for their messianic prophecies (8:13–15, 20–22). He had hoped, in other words, that visibly proven prophecies would direct his audience toward prophecies whose fulfillment remains *un*seen. Perhaps, he reasoned, by being shown their wickedness and mentioning the Messiah, the people might take those two data points in conjunction and turn to repentance. Instead, the Nephites ignore any mention of the Messiah, grow angry at the revelation of their wickedness, and become obsessed with Nephi$_2$ himself. Some insist that "he is a good man" (verse 7), while others accuse him of being a coconspirator in the assassination (9:20), and still others make him an object of superstition (verse 41). Rather than recognizing themselves in Nephi$_2$'s prophetic mirror, the Nephites either grow angry at their reflection or obsess over the sparkle of its miraculous frame.

As with any good mirror, however, labels can't seem to attach to Nephi$_2$. He reflects back to the people a variety of faces, depending on the assumptions each person brought to the encounter in the first place. As in Helaman 1, here again we see the Nephites splitting three ways: those who believe Nephi$_2$ (verse 39), those who identify him as a prophet (verse 40), and those who call him a god (verse 41). Nephi$_2$ has functioned so effectively as a mirrored surface that the people can't agree on how to identify him. Instead, all appellations simply refract to the schisms among the people until, enthralled in their own conflict, the people forget Nephi₂ altogether: "It came to pass that there arose a division among the people, insomuch that they divided hither and thither and went their ways, leaving Nephi alone, as he was standing in the midst of them" (10:1).

*the sealing power*

Just as the Nephites find themselves once again in a three-way conflict, Nephi₂ too shows signs of returning to where he started. Mulling over recent events and still "much cast down because of the wickedness of the people" (Hel. 10:3), Nephi₂ "went his way towards his own house" (verse 2). He doesn't get far, however. A divine voice stops him to deliver an unannounced blessing: "Blessed art thou, Nephi, for those things which thou hast done; for I have beheld how thou hast with unwearyingness declared the word, which I have given unto thee, unto this people" (verse 4). This merciful endorsement of Nephi₂ at the very moment he feels most dejected is noteworthy for its compassion, but closer inspection reveals further significant details in the Lord's opening words to his prophet.

First, Helaman 10:4 is a clear quotation of 1 Nephi 2:1, in which father Lehi is also "blessed...[for] the things which [he] hast done," namely, "declar[ing]" God's word "unto this people." The Lord's endorsement thus carries an ominous undertone: Nephi₂ may be "blessed," but the echo of 1 Nephi 2 suggests that the Nephites are in a situation as precarious as was Jerusalem just prior to the Babylonian destruction. Second, in a book intently focused on the theme of sight, it is striking that God warrants his blessing in terms of what he has seen: "Blessed art thou, Nephi,...for I have beheld" (verse 4). God, too, has a gaze pertinent to the book of Helaman, and he's on the lookout for servants living orthogonal to the usual self-seeking that characterizes humanity. Notice, for instance, how the Lord commends Nephi$_2$: "Thou hast not feared [this people], and hast not sought thine own life" (Hel. 10:4). Nephi$_2$, in other words, has been oriented neither by fear of others nor by fear for himself. Having avoided the binary of typical human concerns, Nephi$_2$'s difference has allowed him to seek for aims that are largely invisible among the Nephites at present. Rather than wealth or power or a secure future, God reports, Nephi$_2$ has "sought my will, and to keep my commandments" (verse 4). Whatever follows in this divine speech, we must remember that it is framed first as a blessing to Nephi$_2$ for his diligence and that God's gaze seeks out those whose faces are oriented toward him in turn.

Because Nephi$_2$ is stable and righteously aligned, God grants him power to stabilize and align others—or, at least, other *things*. Helaman 10 is famous for being the chapter in which Nephi$_2$ is given the sealing power. Curiously, however, the power Nephi$_2$ receives bears very little resemblance to what most Latter-day Saints understand sealing to be. Far from helping Nephi$_2$ establish a church in Jesus's absence (see Matt. 16:18–19) or extending family relationships into the eternities, Nephi$_2$ is told that he will use this power "according to the wickedness of this people" (Hel. 10:6), apparently as a tool of punishment and rebuke. "I will make thee mighty in word and in deed, in faith and in works," promises the Lord, "yea, even that all things shall be done unto thee according to thy word" (verse 5). Nephi$_2$'s sealing power thus sutures words to actions rather than fathers to sons or wives to husbands. It becomes a way of bringing things into correspondence and making sure that when Nephi$_2$ speaks something, its effects will be brought about. Here, again, the Lord reminds Nephi$_2$ that this suturing is a response to Nephi$_2$'s proven constancy: "For thou shalt not ask that which is contrary to my will" (verse 5). Because Nephi$_2$ is in alignment with God, he is given power for his words to align with earthly effects. The consequence, then, is that Nephi$_2$'s sealing power functions as yet another kind of mirroring—this time making heaven mirror earth: "Behold, . . . whatsoever ye shall seal on earth shall be sealed in heaven; and whatsoever ye shall loose on earth shall be loosed in heaven" (verse 7). And lest readers misunderstand that this places Nephi$_2$ in some metaphysical realm beyond the concerns of the everyday, the Lord adds, "And thus shall ye have power among *this* people" (verse 7; emphasis added). Like Nephi$_2$'s prophecies in the previous chapters, the sealing power is also meant to be a mirror put in the service of making something visible to the Nephites.

In what way, however, could this tool be useful among a nation so far mired in sin and depravity? What good can be accomplished among the Nephites by forcing the efficacy of mere words? On closer inspection it's nevertheless clear that "mere words" might be precisely the right site of intervention. We might notice, for instance, that words are notoriously unreliable in the book of Helaman. Secret combinations engage in manipulative speech and slippery oaths, constantly bathing their language in duplicity. While words come unhinged from reality among the Nephites, Nephi$_2$ is given a sure footing and the power to tie words back down to their referents. We might also remember Nephi$_2$'s predicament following his sermon. At this point in their story, the Nephites are hopelessly unstable, caught up in fantasies and illusions and constantly slipping out from under the sight of their own condemnation. If he is to make any headway, Nephi$_2$ needs something unmistakable and unavoidable to grab their attention. At a moment when everything is falling apart, when people and wealth are slippery and everything merely refracts off of him and his prophetic word, Nephi$_2$ can make good use of a power that steadies and holds together.

This is what he had tried to do with his two signs—after all, what could be more arresting and forceful than murder?—and yet the Nephites still managed to squirm out from under their implications. Nephi$_2$'s last resort, it seems, is to create a situation similar to that in Helaman 4 in which the people come face to face with the consequences of their unrighteous living *and* have no way to escape the sight. Though Nephi$_2$ has been clearly reflecting their situation back at them, they've nevertheless slipped away by distracting themselves with minor squabbles or political concerns. This, it seems, is what the sealing power corrects. Armed with an ability to suture words to outcomes, Nephi$_2$ can manufacture a situation whose existential stakes are so high that the Nephites will be forced to confront the outcome of their wickedness. Indeed, this kind of stakes-raising confrontation seems to be exactly what the Lord has in mind: "Ye shall have power over this people, and shall smite the earth with famine, and with pestilence, and destruction, according to the wickedness of this people" (10:6). As we will see in the next chapter, Nephi$_2$ takes the Lord very much at his word.

Though the sealing power in Helaman 10 is intended as one more tool in Nephi$_2$'s mirroring arsenal, and despite its differences from other scriptural instances of sealing, it nevertheless provides a model for how Latter-day Saints understand sealing today. Just as Nephi$_2$ stabilizes the correspondence between words and things against the moral decay among the

Nephites, Latter-day Saint sealings stabilize family relationships against the decay of death. To counter the visible connections by which the world falsely adjudicates relationships—money, power, prestige, and so on—the sealing power supplements with a series of invisible threads that knit hearts together in new ways. Sealing is as invisible as it is stabilizing, and given the themes of the book of Helaman, we should not be surprised to see those two qualities going hand in hand. We will be stable to the degree that we anchor ourselves to foundations that the world cannot see and orient around metrics that the world cannot understand. The more we draw earth into correspondence with heaven, the steadier we will be.

*a final word on mirroring*

If Helaman 9 ended with Nephi$_2$ becoming opaque to the Nephites, Helaman 10 ends with Nephi$_2$ becoming opaque to readers. Though we had been privy to Nephi$_2$'s innermost emotions throughout most of chapter III (his "agony of...soul" [7:6], his careful appraisal of audience dynamics [8:10], his "being much cast down" [10:3]), as soon as Nephi$_2$ receives the sealing power, readers lose all access to his interiority. His thoughts and feelings no longer rise to the surface of the narrative and he becomes, instead, an enigmatic, incomprehensible, quasimystical prophet. Though he had been part of the political establishment, like his father before him, now he stands entirely outside of it. Though he was a judge-turned-preacher on the familiar model of Alma (right down to miraculous prison scenes!), now he is a preacher of a very different cast. This time around, when the people attempt to throw him in prison (10:15), the outcome is very different: "The power of God was with him...for he was taken by

the Spirit and conveyed away out of the midst of them"
(verse 16). Where Helaman 8 portrayed Nephi$_2$ as a
speaking prophet on the order of Isaiah or Jeremiah, by
Helaman 10 he becomes a supernatural prophet more
on the order of Elijah or Jesus, sealing the heavens (Hel.
11) and being whisked about by the spirit.

In a way, then, Nephi$_2$ becomes a kind of mirror for
readers as well. Just as his prophecy emulated secret
combinations and his signs reflected Nephite violence,
now his opacity functions as a mirror for us. What do
we make of this enigmatic prophet? What kind of story
do we tell about him in the spaces left by such sparse
textual detail? How we fill in these narrative gaps tells
us much more about ourselves than it does about
Nephi$_2$. If we nevertheless find ourselves struggling to
get a handle on Nephi$_2$ himself, as the chapter closes,
we can take comfort that doing so was never the point
of Mormon's chapter III. In Nephi$_2$'s opacity, Mormon
presents readers with an opportunity to see something
about *themselves*. Indeed, this chapter can be read as
one long exploration of the role of prophets and the
sorts of mirrors they hold up. Why is *mirroring* Nephi$_2$'s
preferred tactic for addressing secret combinations?
And what might chapter III reveal about a people's relationship with its prophets?

In some ways, the most astonishing moment of the
original chapter III occurs right at the beginning, when
the people stand confused around a weeping prophet,
unable to figure out where his lament is coming from.
"Who could possibly think anything's wrong?" we can
imagine them wondering. In their bewilderment at the
figure of a grieving leader, the Nephites reveal their
complete inability to see themselves. They see a former chief judge inexplicably baring his soul on a tower
amid signs of unprecedented economic prosperity, but

they utterly fail to see the truth of their behavior or how it has led to the tears now watering Nephi₂'s garden. Like these Nephites, then, anytime we find ourselves wondering why a prophet would say *that*, of all things, there's good reason to take a long, hard look in the mirror.

The original chapter III serves as Mormon's reminder that our relationship with the invisible must be more like the relationship we have with a mirror than with a magnifying glass. When the book of Helaman challenges us to attend to what is hidden, it has something especially invisible in mind: ourselves. A mirror, remember, does not compare and contrast two objects; instead, it reveals the traits of one. The person who stares back at you in a mirror is your twin, your own self rendered into an object and presented to you for inspection. Likewise, Nephi₂'s sermon does not compare the Nephites with some other group in order to shed light on both, as a straightforward comparison would do. Rather, he sets the Nephites against themselves, not unlike the way Jesus constantly turns questions back on the people who ask them ("How readest *thou*?" [Luke 10:26], "What think *ye*?" [Matt. 21:28], "Whom say *ye* that I am?" [Matt. 16:15]). In the same way, the visibility the book of Helaman aims to give readers is not the visibility of a searchlight but the visibility of our own reflection.

Mirrors serve many uses—they are aids to personal grooming, of course, but they are also tools for safety, entertainment, and scientific inquiry. Some mirrors expand our range of vision (the side mirrors on a car or the mirrors in a parking garage). Others can distort and project images (fun house mirrors). Still others help us focus on what is invisibly distant (mirrors in telescopes) or use our tools with greater precision (mirrors that aim lasers for eye surgery and precision welding). In each case, a mirror reflects an image in order to train our sight in a new direction or reveal something we would otherwise be unable to see. Chapter III is the story of a prophet trying mirror after mirror, hoping to find the exact size and shape of glass that will focus the Nephites' eyes in the right direction. Which mirror will reflect their sin, reveal their blind spots, and guide them to safety? Which glass will help them see themselves with the least distortion? Nephi$_2$ holds up a mirror to the Nephites in as many ways as possible, and when they still manage to escape its force, God grants him the ability to make heaven mirror earth so he can try yet again.

There is a reason that one of Paul's most potent images for the life of discipleship is looking in a mirror with varying degrees of clarity. "Now we see through a glass, darkly," he writes, "but then face to face" (1 Cor. 13:12). "Glass," however, is an unfortunate translation, and misses all the reflective force of the Greek word *esoptron*, or "mirror." Mortal life, explains Paul, is the equivalent of a tarnished mirror seeking polish and clarity. We hope one day to see ourselves reflected clearly in its glass and, even more, to see a second face residing in the familiar curves of our own—what Alma describes as receiving God's image in our countenances (Alma 5:14). We won't be ready to see the face of God until we've spent a lifetime studying our own, learning intimately all its blemishes and sun spots, and until we've spent more time creating laugh lines or drying tears than applying makeup or styling our hair. Do our mirrors sharpen our vision, or do we take false comfort in the reflections of distorted glass? We ought to select mirrors that will magnify our warts and wrinkles, helping us see that we are not as consecrated as

we think, not as generous to the poor, never as gracious and forgiving and tender as we hope. The gospel is precisely such a mirror, a tool designed for self-reflection and repentance. If we weaponize those mirrors against others rather than turning them thoughtfully on ourselves, we can be sure that we have fallen into the same distortions that characterize the Nephites in the book of Helaman.

# IV

## Helaman 11–12

When the original chapter IV begins, we find Nephi₂ still on the scene. His story isn't over yet despite the fact that, curiously, it *will* be over very shortly. In a mere eighteen verses, Nephi₂ will disappear from the book of Helaman almost entirely. Readers must thus begin chapter IV with the following question: Why is there a chapter break *here*, of all places? If all that remains of Nephi₂'s activity in the book of Helaman is a handful of verses, why not tack those onto the end of the previous chapter and send readers on to the next scene, no strings attached? The answer, I want to suggest, is in line with the characteristic pessimism of the book of Helaman. As in previous chapters, Mormon is doing everything he can to make sure readers don't understand Nephi₂'s story as having a happy ending. From his perspective, there is nothing happy about the aftermath of Nephi₂'s intervention among the Nephites, despite a few signs of early optimism. In order to train readers to see in the right way, then, Mormon must break his story in odd places, adding different conclusions to reveal what's actually going on among the people.

The original chapter IV opens on a sharp descent into total chaos. The people may have initially divided around Nephi₂ on just one road in a single city, but that local, relatively minor division escalates into national violence. "The contentions" left over at the end of Helaman 10 only "increase," until it's a matter of outright "wars" (Hel. 11:1). The culprits, predictably, are secret combinations (verse 2). Despite all the miracles and prophecies that have intervened between the opening of the book and now, the situation has only worsened. Nephi$_2$'s interventional tactics must also increase with the scale of the crisis. His first instinct is to replace civil war with famine, and so he takes to his knees: "O Lord, do not suffer that this people shall be destroyed by the sword;...rather let there be a famine in the land" (verse 4). This constitutes Nephi$_2$'s first reported exercise of the sealing power, and, interestingly, he shows some nervousness about implementing that power. Rather than directly commanding the earth (as the Lord had suggested [10:8–10]), Nephi$_2$ issues a request to God, and he also keeps noticeably within the precedents the Lord had set—it was, after all, the divine voice who suggested "smit[ing] the earth with famine" as the first on a list of examples of how this sealing might be used (verse 6).

If Nephi$_2$ *is* nervous about wielding divine power, there is nothing tentative or inexperienced about selecting famine to replace war. Against the people's violent insistence on turning one another into enemies, Nephi$_2$ arrays a trial calculated to bond the people instead—albeit at horrifying cost. Hunger is both a great unifier and an effective way to disrupt rivalries. Vilifying others doesn't seem so important when your gut is gnawed with cravings, just as killing enemy women and children loses priority when your own family begs you to find food. In short, famine promises to bring the people face to face with death itself, reminiscent of the military standstill of Helaman 4. The Nephites have spent too long planting bodies in the ground and watering the earth with blood; engaged as they are in a violent imitation of agricultural life, perhaps it is only a literal agricultural failure that can bring them to their senses.

Though it takes the better part of two years and exacts a horrific death toll, Nephi$_2$'s plan initially seems to work: "The people saw that they were about to perish by famine, and they began to remember the Lord their God; and they began to remember the words of Nephi" (11:7). Unfortunately, like so much else in Helaman, this outcome seems optimistic only on its surface. Close attention reveals a different story. To begin with, notice that the people "remember the Lord" only in the abstract; nothing is said about their relationship to the *words* of the Lord. The only words they seem to remember are "the words of Nephi," but this memory, too, is suspect. Verse 8 specifies which words, in particular, capture their attention: "all the words which thou hast spoken concerning our destruction." Captivated only by the likelihood of their own demise, the people seem to have forgotten that Nephi$_2$ said anything about a Messiah or about their relationship to prophets. Notice, too, that the only words they remember are misattributed! Nephi$_2$'s announcement of impending destruction was the very pronouncement ascribed to God: "Except ye repent, *thus saith the Lord*, ye shall be smitten even unto destruction" (10:14, emphasis added; see also verse 11). The Nephites' selective listening transfers the oracle of destruction from the Lord to Nephi$_2$ and allows them to conveniently forget that Nephi$_2$ said anything else of importance, thus insulating the people from the very Lord they purport to remember.

The Nephites seem to forget that the Lord is someone with whom they can communicate directly and someone who has communicated with them in the past. Since Nephi$_2$ is the one with the "words," it's no surprise that the people beg *him* to act as their divine intermediary. Prompted by the people (11:8), Nephi$_2$

petitions the Lord a second time, now trying to end the famine he'd begun a few verses earlier (verses 12–13). He marshals evidence of the people's repentance, noting their apparent piety and their suppression of the Gadianton robbers (verses 10–11), but despite Nephi$_2$'s positive spin on the situation, readers might have several questions. For one thing, this prayer is very different from the prayer offered in verse 4. Though Nephi$_2$ initiated the famine with a prayer that spans only a single verse (verse 4), his later request for rain takes seven (verses 10–16). Why does the start of the famine require so few words while the end of the famine requires so many? And why, for that matter, does Nephi$_2$ seem more tentative and anxious? The second prayer is full of self-effacing requests ("wilt thou," in verses 11, 12, 13, 16) rather than imperatives ("do not" and "let there be," in verse 4). Has Nephi$_2$ been chastened by the enormous death toll of the famine he instigated? Is he worried about venturing beyond the examples God suggested in Helaman 10?

Though both of these are possibilities, Mormon's editorializing around this prayer recommends one other likelihood: Nephi$_2$ may be subconsciously aware that he's asking preemptively, that the people's repentance isn't as wholehearted as they pretend. Nephi$_2$ may be trying to convince himself as much as he's trying to convince God. For all the data that Nephi$_2$ attempts to marshal in support of his claim that "they have repented" (11:15), it is never historically corroborated by Mormon. When Nephi$_2$ reports that "this people repenteth" (verse 10), Mormon does not sweep in with statistical data about church growth or anecdotes of increased care for the poor; and when Nephi$_2$ insists that "they have swept away the band of Gadianton from amongst them" (verse 10), Mormon refuses to give any of the backstory that he usually relishes. This supposed eradication of the Gadianton robbers is neither narrated nor confirmed, and the consequence is that Nephi$_2$'s second prayer is editorially marked with an enormous asterisk. Nephi$_2$ may think secret combinations have been eradicated and that the Nephites are on the upswing, but Mormon knows better.

From Mormon's perspective, then, Nephi's assurance that the people "have repented" is based on personal optimism and limited data. The Nephites have mourned and admitted Nephi$_2$'s prophetic power (verse 8) in such a way that he understandably thinks them to be sincere. But Mormon signals to readers that this so-called repentance is largely just an eagerness for an end to the famine. Like all prophets through the ages, Nephi$_2$ is burdened with loving and serving a people who never quite live up to his aspirations for them, who fall short of what he's taught, and who are prone to halfway repentance in order to obtain life-easing blessings. By leaving his doubts expressed through silence rather than outright critique, Mormon leaves room for Nephi$_2$'s generosity while simultaneously alerting readers that here, too, there is no reason for optimism.

At any rate, God proves as generous as his prophet and the requested rain is given (verse 17). Naturally, the Nephites are ecstatic (verse 18) and begin to celebrate Nephi$_2$. The prophet who months before had been a source of derision and then division, and then had acted as an intermediary to a vengeful deity, now becomes a celebrated public figure (verse 18). Readers might well roll their eyes at the convenience of now accepting a prophet who gives the people exactly what they want. It's also telling that the people celebrate Nephi$_2$ in such overwrought terms. Calling him a "great prophet" (verse 18), they echo similarly overwrought language used to describe the chief judge at his funeral in Helaman 9 where, though the people assembled to memorialize their "great chief judge who had been slain" (9:10), they immediately betrayed that zeal by proving only too happy to interrupt the proceedings with a legal trial.

All this suggests that the Nephites relate to authority figures in an aggrandizing way. They fixate on the spectacular and celebrate the falsely inflated but then betray themselves with quick distraction from the very thing they claim to commemorate. Just as no one seemed *really* to care about the "great chief judge" and the people were easily distracted by the chance to cross-examine Nephi$_2$, the similarly overwrought description of Nephi$_2$ as a "great prophet" hints that the people are on their way to another distraction. It's human nature that language grows overembellished when it's compensating for a lack of real grounding. We cover personal weaknesses or relationship problems by talking endlessly about our strengths or projecting images of domestic perfection. The Nephites, for their part, hide indifference to government authority and prophetic power by loudly professing their admiration for chief judges and "great prophets." The real test, of course, is whether or not those laws are obeyed in private or whether one thanks God in prayer for prophetic words. The best commendation we can give a prophet, after all, is to take his words seriously. Verbose, dazzling, public display risks becoming a cover because the real thing—real devotion, real piety, real humility—never needs to be dressed up.

It's in this tone, then, that we might hear the very next verse of the chapter—a curious note that has long puzzled readers. Right as the people are hoisting Nephi$_2$ onto their shoulders, the camera pulls back to reveal someone else: "And behold, Lehi, his brother, was not a whit behind him as to things pertaining to righteousness" (11:19). Lehi$_2$ is not part of this public exultation and yet he is still "not a whit behind." Though the Nephites are focused only on one prophet—the more prominent, sign-giving one who has recently satisfied their preference—the text, at the price of considerable narrative awkwardness, slips in mention of a quiet brother who has been working behind the scenes all along. Mormon wants to remind readers that grand miracles and shows of strength are not the proper indicator of success in God's kingdom, despite the Nephites' taste for such things.

This mention of Lehi$_2$ also serves as a reminder not to view Nephi$_2$ through the lens projected onto him by the people. Though people misunderstand Nephi$_2$ to be primarily an oracle whom they can petition for good weather and plentiful harvests, Nephi$_2$'s proper parallel is his brother, his partner in ministry and quiet, unpopular righteousness. By pairing Nephi$_2$ with his virtually invisible brother, a character so consistently overlooked by the text, Mormon encourages readers to hold Nephi$_2$ apart from the Nephites' assessment of him and to keep our attention trained on what's *not* seen, what's *not* flashy. It is someone quietly righteous, like Lehi$_2$, who serves as our proper model of faithfulness, and Nephi$_2$ belongs to *that* world of gentle, unassuming devotion rather than the world into which the Nephites are trying to absorb him.

Once the Nephites are no longer threatened with imminent death, they get back to the same old work of expansion and economic growth. Waste places are rebuilt, territory expands, and the people multiply "until they...cover the whole face of the land" (11:20). This time around, their expansion includes a religious component ("the church did spread throughout the face of all the land" [verse 21]), but there are early signs that something is amiss even here: there arose "a few contentions concerning the points of doctrine" (verse

22). Even the church fails to be the kind of peaceful fraternal order it is supposed to be and finds itself rent with internal conflict. The problem is less, it seems, that false beliefs have crept into the church and more that the resolution of those errors causes "contentions." Focused on affirming correct doctrine, the people overlook the division their focus creates. Whether fighting over succession or fighting over doctrine, the Nephites' eagerness for schisms reads ominously. Sure enough, it takes only three years and as many verses before a group of dissenters abscond to Lamanite territory and rile up an army (verse 24).

Readers find themselves back in the same place, watching as the Nephites, with exhausting monotony, engage in the same old behaviors. The only difference between Helaman 11 and Helaman 1 is that everything has been dangerously scaled up. Now the dissenter-led Lamanite army *becomes* the secret combination, "retreat[ing] back into the mountains" and deliberately seeking out Gadianton plans (verses 25–26). For the first time in the book of Helaman, secret combinations constitute an external threat large enough and visible enough to be challenged militarily. The Nephites are forced to send "an army of strong men . . . upon the mountains to search out this band of robbers" (verse 28). They are rebuffed in short order, however, and "obliged to return . . . unto their own lands" (verse 31). It is now clear that Nephi$_2$'s attempt to replace war with famine did little good. Within a few short years, the Nephites are right back where they started. Because things among the Nephites are scaling up to unprecedented levels, the size of the mirror reflecting them needs to scale up, too. The Nephites' crisis is too large to be adequately rendered by individual prophets or small families. It's time, in other words, for metaphors on a whole new order of magnitude.

*the earth*

Right when things start careening wildly out of control, Mormon takes an unexpected step back from the narration. Though Nephite instability and blindness are reaching their most extreme, he veers toward what can only appear as a non sequitur. Mormon interrupts his story with news about—of all things!—the earth. Most of Helaman 12 is a hymn celebrating the earth's ability to shift and rearrange at the command of its creator. God can move the planet with a word (verse 13), dry up oceans with a thought (verse 16), and turn the very ground against the men who are accustomed to finding it reliable (verse 18). The extremity of the Nephites' crisis has now escalated to such a scale that Mormon recruits the entire globe to make their predicament visible for readers. In fact, when we look at Helaman's other chapters, we find hints that Mormon has been using this tactic all along. The earth is profoundly unstable throughout the book of Helaman; from earthquakes and trembling prison walls to soil that swallows buried treasures, the earth is an uncanny mirror of Nephite instability. The book of Helaman uses the earth as a metaphor for the unstable and shifting place of the Nephites in relation to the Lamanites, to God, and to each other. What better mirror for mortal flaws could there be, after all, than the very dust out of which mankind was formed?

Not only has Mormon hit upon a new metaphor to aid his lessons in visibility, but the text implies that he's hit upon a new source, as well. Mormon is not known for writing in lyrical tones, and yet Helaman 12 is full of parallelism and powerful vocatives ("O how foolish," "O how great," "for behold," and so on [verses 4–8]). The stakes of this poetic expansion are also more cosmic than Mormon's predilection for down-to-earth historical detail—the entire globe upends its trajectory (verses 14–15) or dramatic curses overtake all of humanity (verses 18–21). And when God is described in this chapter, he takes on a decidedly ancient guise as a nature deity known primarily through earthquakes and cosmic phenomena. It's as if Mormon has discovered an ancient hymn about the earth's motility and inserted it into the chapter as a set piece for his drama.

This poem also recommends itself to Mormon's editorial project because it serves as a perfect interlude between the two prophets (Nephi$_2$ and Samuel) who both diagnose Nephite instability and enlist the earth's help in correcting it. Recall that Nephi$_2$ instituted a famine, quite literally calling the earth to revolt against the people. Samuel, as well, will give a sign that involves the planet moving outside its normal bounds and issue a curse on hidden treasures, two themes that occur explicitly in this poem (verses 14–15, 18–19). In addition to bridging resonant themes between Nephi$_2$ and Samuel, this hymn also fits perfectly with the current situation of the Nephites. The poem is preceded by a lament over "how quick" the Nephites are "to do iniquity, and how slow to do good" (verses 4–5). The people may move "quickly" and "slowly" to varying degrees but, like the earth in this poem, they're always in motion.

To help us get a handle on this hymn's theological message, it's best to begin with its organization and its logic. The hymn can be broken up into two large chunks: a first half focused on the earth (verses 9–17) and a second, smaller portion dealing with man and his "treasure" (verses 18–22). Within those two broad halves, the hymn proceeds in a series of pairs according to whom or to what God's voice is addressed, with two editorial asides interspersed after each group of three (see FIGURE 4).

There is also a clear logic to the hymn's progression, moving from small surface phenomena to colossal

Hills and mountains quake (verse 9)
Hills and mountains broken up (verse 10)

God's voice shakes the earth (verse 11)
God's voice rocks the earth's foundation (verse 12)

To the earth (verse 13)
To the earth (verse 14)

   Comment/aside: Heliocentric model (verse 15)

To the waters (verse 16)
To the mountain (verse 17)

About a treasure (verse 18)
To a treasure (verse 19)

To a man (verse 20)
To a man (verse 21)

   Comment/aside: Transition to repentance (verse 22)

FIGURE 4  Series of pairs in hymn from Helaman 12:9–21.

motion at the very center of the earth. The text begins, first, with mention of "the dust" that lies on the earth's surface (verse 8) followed by reports about "hills and mountains" that "tremble and quake" (verse 9) until their vibrations intensify and "they are broken up" altogether (verse 10). It's as though minor surface phenomena are picking up intensity, reverberating through larger and larger scales of earthly motion. Indeed, the next verses mention "the whole earth shak[ing]" (verses 11–12) until, in the following passage, the earth "is moved" out of its orbit entirely (verses 13–15). What began as just a few grains of dust shifting imperceptibly gives way over the course of seven verses to a complete disruption of the planet's orbit.

The hymn's content is just as important as its form, of course, and a number of theological lessons lie behind this curious interlude in Helaman 12. For instance, this poem contains one of the most puzzling verses of the entire Book of Mormon. Sometimes called "the Copernican verse," verse 15 portrays a seemingly anachronistic understanding of the heliocentric universe (that is, a model in which the planets rotate around the sun). Any study of this verse must also note, however, that it contributes directly to the logic of the passage and exemplifies the theme of visibility that animates the book of Helaman. Mormon writes, "According to [God's] word the earth goeth back, and it appeareth unto man that the sun standeth still; yea, and behold, this is so; for surely it is the earth that moveth and not the sun" (verse 15). Just as in preceding verses, this passage shows God speaking to the earth and effecting its movement. The verse means less to draw attention to cutting-edge astronomical knowledge several hundred years in advance of Galileo and more to emphasize that in this instance, just like the others, God's voice is moving the earth, specifically, rather than the sun.

In the process, however, Mormon's comment also returns us to the theme of visibility by contrasting the way the situation "appeareth unto man" with what "is so" in reality. When the day lengthens out and the earth removes out of its orbit, he explains, it appears to mankind "that the sun standeth still." Despite the evidence of their eyes, however, "it is the earth that moveth and not the sun" (verse 15). The earth's movement thus serves as a mirror of planetary reality in a way that is not immediately visible from our perspective on the earth's surface. Humankind fails to see the motion of the earth simply because it's too immediate, because it concerns the very ground under their feet. Readers should hear echoes, here, of the regular drumbeat of the book of Helaman: human perception is faulty, prone to distraction by what is distant and flashy, and oblivious to what is invisible precisely for its nearness and ubiquity. Keep those eyes focused on what is most proximate to you, Mormon reminds us. While our eyes are focused on the shiny and spectacular and distant, God intervenes at the level of the mundane and invisible and local.

For such a brief poetic interlude, Helaman 12 also bears a number of parallels to King Benjamin's homily from Mosiah 2. Both texts compare man's nothingness to "the dust of the earth" (Hel. 12:7; Mosiah 2:25–26), plead for the repentance of their audience in the face of eternal judgment (Hel. 12:24–25; Mosiah 2:38–40), and include key terminology such as "boast" and "wisdom" (Hel. 12:5; Mosiah 2:17, 24). The two passages also describe God as a heavenly king (Hel. 12:6; Mosiah 2:19) and share an interest in the paradoxical ways God blesses his undeserving children (Hel. 12:2; Mosiah 2:22–25). If the text's structure and tone were meant to imply that Mormon is incorporating an ancient source, the text's content suggests that he modifies that source after the pattern of King Benjamin.

Perhaps the largest connection between Helaman 12 and Mosiah 2, however, is both texts' investment in creation. Much of Helaman 12 centers on the way natural landscapes respond to God's voice. For those acquainted with Genesis 1, this should be familiar territory. Just as God called creation into being by the power of his word, he now dictates that hills, mountains, and rivers break out of their natural order. And just as the creation story in Genesis culminates with the appearance of man and God's explicit instructions to Adam and Eve (Gen. 1:26–28), Helaman 12 also culminates with a turn toward human beings and God speaking directly to them in tones eerily reminiscent of the fall: "Because of thine iniquities thou shalt be cut off from my presence" (verse 21). Though Benjamin is not as focused on the natural landscape as is Helaman 12, he is also minutely attuned to creation—in particular, to the mercy conveyed by God's creation of humankind (Mosiah 2:20–21). And though that createdness combines with God's routine care to make us "unprofitable servants" (Mosiah 2:21), it's clear that Benjamin views this relationship as good news, leading to the most profound sermon on grace in the entire Latter-day Saint canon.

What for Benjamin was a generous, merciful order of creation, however, becomes for Mormon a scene of dejection. Rather than invoking creation as mercy, Mormon instead undoes creation as judgment. Where Genesis 1 carefully secures the foundations of the earth, putting soil, water, and life in order, Helaman 12 instead reports on everything being moved out of its place and every expectation coming undone. It's further clear, based on another connection with Benjamin's sermon, that human wickedness is the root cause of all this collapse. Immediately after outlining God's merciful creation and preservation of humankind, Benjamin names the one simple obligation God enjoins on his people: "He doth require that ye should do as he hath commanded you; for which if ye do, he doth immediately bless you" (Mosiah 2:24). Mormon also makes mention of how God "doth bless and prosper those who put their trust in him" (Hel. 12:1), but this time it comes as a condition rather than a reward: "At the very time when he doth prosper his people, . . . then is the time that they do harden their hearts, and do forget the Lord their God" (verse 2). For Benjamin, *as soon as* you are righteous, God immediately blesses you; for Mormon, however, *as soon as* the people are blessed, they turn wicked. Both texts join God's blessing with the immediacy of some other outcome, but to opposite effect; for Benjamin, this immediacy is a sign of God's goodness and man's indebtedness, whereas for Mormon it's an indication of man's fickleness.

From here, both texts turn immediately to the question of dust, and once again we find Mormon echoing his predecessor in more despairing terms. Because of your dependence on God, writes Benjamin, "ye cannot say that ye are even as much as the dust of the earth" (Mosiah 2:25). Though he implies that we must, therefore, be *less* than the dust, it is notable that Benjamin phrases this gently, negating our equality ("ye cannot say that ye are even") rather than positing our nothingness outright. Mormon, on the other hand, pulls no punches: "O how great is the nothingness of the children of men; yea, even they are less than the dust of the earth"—because the dust, at least, obeys God's commands (Hel. 12:7–8). Where Benjamin intends his mention of "dust" to be gentle and hopeful, Mormon fully intends to condemn human frailty.

In short, Helaman 12 undoes Benjamin's sermon and reverses its trajectory. Where Mosiah 2 began with creation and culminated in man's fraternity with dust, Helaman 12 begins by marking humankind as *less* than the dust, which then gradually begins to vibrate until the whole of creation comes undone after it. It is likely no coincidence that the movements—which culminate in mountains being leveled and the foundation of the earth rocking off balance—begin first on the very surface of the earth, where human beings live and act. It is the surface of the earth—that portion that comes into regular contact with humankind—that first begins to shift and sway. It's where *humankind* touches the earth that the problem begins.

This is how the first thematic half of Helaman 12 connects with the second. If the earth is put in motion because creation is being undone in judgment, it's clear that there is one very specific sin being judged. The second half of the poem focuses on humankind's relationship with wealth. Money, as readers know, is central to Nephite wickedness all through the Book of Mormon. In Helaman alone, it is the paradigmatic blessing that sparks hardened hearts (verse 2), the primary motive of secret combinations, the root of all the economic expansion that drives the Nephites to distraction, and a point of repeated critique for every prophetic voice within its pages. Wealth is flashy and shiny and accommodates the purchase of visible status markers. It is both the root of the Nephite problem and a perfect example of the glitter that draws human eyes in the wrong direction. So far, in Helaman 12, God's voice has been addressed in imperatives to the earth, but only on the subject of money does God begin to issue curses (verses 18–19). And in a chilling turn, that curse on treasure gives way to the only other object of cursing in the chapter: "man" himself. Mankind's relationship with money is so risky that he hazards being "cut off from [God's] presence" to such a degree that "he cannot be saved" (verses 21–22).

This connection between the earth and human greed also bears ready connections with the creation story. Adam and Eve's first recorded act was to grasp after something that was denied to them and to take ownership of a natural resource in an inappropriate way (Gen. 3:6). As a result, both humankind *and* the earth were subject to the fall. This kinship with the earth is part of what makes it such a profound mirror. Adam and Eve found their fallen existence mirrored in the thorns and thistles of the fallen world just as the Nephites find their spiritual instability reflected in the earth's refusal to grant them security in their wealth and in nature's revolt at being liquidated for financial gain. In Genesis as well humanity is figured as a class of gardeners who "dress" and "keep" the land (2:15). In a grotesque distortion of that obligation, the book of Helaman instead reveals the Nephites to be sowing violence, planting bodies, watering the earth with blood, burying up wicked plans, and extracting gold and silver just to return them to the earth again. Is it any wonder that the earth is here depicted revolting against their contempt for Edenic stewardship?

Nor is the earth's revolt merely a poetic theme restricted to the verses of Helaman 12. This chapter ought to feel eerily contemporary because, today as well, there remains disorder in creation. The earth has been economized, vandalized, profligately wasted, and watered with the blood of those sacrificed in conflicts over its material reserves. We readers must also confront our complicity in disappearing rainforests, dying reefs, the plundering of natural landscapes in a rush for oil, and the disregard for people and species all over the globe as the wealthy and powerful rob their land of its resources. If current trends are any indication, the earth risks being wasted by man's poor environmental stewardship long before it risks being wasted by Christ's coming. How different is our environmental instability, our wealth inequality, our corporate greed and our defiance of monetary restraint from what the Nephites display in these chapters? Are we, too, seeking voraciously after wealth, hoping to secure our future in fiscal rather than spiritual terms? Do we lust after proofs of our cosmopolitanism, after international vacations or exotic travels, after the right size of home and the right brand of clothing? All these, we might notice, are practices in spectacle and public visibility, and all come at the expense of the earth.

Is it any wonder that Helaman 12 shows the earth jumping at the chance to respond to God's voice rather than man's? And is it any wonder that Mormon can survey a scene such as this only with profound despair? At the close of the original chapter IV, he tries to rally himself to one last note of hope but finds it unsustainable. He can close his interlude only in these words: "I would that all men might be saved. But we read that in the great and last day there are some who shall be cast out, . . . yea, who shall be consigned to a state of endless misery. . . . And thus it is. Amen" (12:25–26).

# V

## Helaman 13–16

The reader is accustomed, by this point, to unprecedented sights within Helaman's pages, but the original chapter V gives us something truly never before seen in the Book of Mormon: a Lamanite prophet. Never before have the Nephites been wicked enough to attract a prophet from outside their nation, and never before have the Lamanites been consistently righteous enough to provide one. Never before has the economy allowed Lamanites and Nephites to freely enter one another's territory (Hel. 6:8). And, just as surprising, readers find the book's first Lamanite preacher to be far more theologically sophisticated, rhetorically compelling, and precise in his prophecies than they might have expected. Once again, the book of Helaman shows us just how much we've tended to leave unseen in our reading, and our guide through this final lesson in visibility is none other than Samuel the Lamanite.

Samuel is introduced as a foil to Nephi$_2$. Beyond their analogous role as the two preachers who conclude the book, a whole rash of other textual details put Samuel and Nephi$_2$ side by side. Both are returning home when they are interrupted by a divine commission (10:12; 13:2–3). Each prophet delivers two signs (9:24–25; 14:2, 14), prophesies of a coming Messiah (8:13–24; 14:2, 12–19), and ventriloquizes the language of their listeners (9:27–34; 13:25). Both call on the Nephites to "repent ye, repent ye" (7:17; 14:19) warning, "It shall be better for the Lamanites than for you" (7:23; 15:14). And just as

Nephi$_2$ curses the earth with famine, Samuel famously announces that "a curse shall come upon the land" in the shape of slippery treasures (13:17–19). Parallels continue to pile up even after the sermons conclude: each prophet causes a division among the people (10:1; 16:1–2), is described in supernatural terms (Nephi is a "god," Samuel has a "devil," in 9:41 and 16:6, respectively), and is protected by "the Spirit" (10:16; 16:2). Finally, both exit the narrative together; the text's last mention of Nephi$_2$ occurs just two verses before Samuel's exit from Zarahemla (16:5, 7–8).

As narrative foils, however, the differences between the two are just as instructive. Where Nephi$_2$'s preaching prioritized the contemporary consequences of Nephite wickedness, Samuel focuses on the future calamities that await the people. While Nephi$_2$'s signs were local, political, and focused on the Nephites, Samuel's signs are cosmic—apocalyptic, even—and primarily concerned with the Messiah. It's also curious that Samuel seems largely uninterested in the Gadianton robbers, whereas Nephi$_2$ shaped his entire intervention around secret combinations. As a result, because Samuel isn't shackled by the sociopolitical concerns that consumed Nephi$_2$, he has room to focus more on the coming Christ in a way Nephi$_2$ seems unable to do. Mormon clearly hopes that a shared picture will come into focus between these two prophets, but if Nephi$_2$ gave us something like a fine zoom on Nephite life, Samuel provides readers with a wide-angle lens.

When compared with Nephi$_2$, Samuel is clearly not a well-known public figure or a member of an elite family; he is an anonymous citizen of a former enemy nation characterized by the Nephites as wicked and backward. Because he is socially invisible to the Nephites, however, Samuel can see things about the people that even Nephi$_2$ was unable to register. Samuel's inclusion in this prophetic duo reminds us that divine messengers and vital perspectives often emerge right out of our blind spot, and that it sometimes takes an outsider to help us hear the voice of God.

*seeing oneself, seeing others*
Samuel begins his foray into Nephite blindness with a shocking pronouncement. Before we are even one verse into his words, we learn that the Nephites face complete annihilation in four hundred years (Hel. 13:5). Though the Nephites are blind to the catastrophic trajectory of their current behavior, Samuel can see it coming a mile off, and he opens his sermon by portending Nephite annihilation for the first time in the large plates. Failing to see every local indication of their wicked trajectory (such as those presented in Nephi$_2$'s sermon, for instance), the Nephites are now forced to see where all this blindness will ultimately land them. Samuel's prophecy of a four-hundred-years-off destruction is less about forestalling the predicted catastrophe, in other words, and more about making visible where the Nephites currently stand.

Unsurprisingly, the first problem singled out for review is the people's relationship to wealth. Nephite greed has progressed so far that Samuel issues a now-unavoidable consequence for their behavior: "Behold, a curse shall come upon the land....Whoso shall hide up treasures in the earth shall find them again no more" (verses 17–18). The Nephites have spent decades hiding themselves from the law and from the consequences of their behavior, and soon, it seems, their penchant for hiding things will extend all the way to their possessions. God, however, is not having it. When the people hide their wealth underground, God promises to call on the very soil to revolt. Every attempt to secure themselves or their future through money will fail, and the earth, whose resources have been stripped for personal gain, will become an instrument of retribution. Samuel clarifies the cause behind this curse in verse 22: "Ye do not remember the Lord your God in the things with which he hath blessed you, but ye do always remember your riches, [but] not to thank the Lord your God for them." In their distraction with the gleam and sparkle of the gift, the people have lost sight of the giver. They cannot tear their eyes away from the glitter of coins and exciting fluctuations in markets and status symbols available for purchase. The visible economy, marked and funded by wealth, is the only economy the Nephites are willing to see.

Naturally, this monetary obsession bleeds into every other realm of Nephite life, including things religious and spiritual. The Nephites "cast out the prophets, and do mock them" (verse 24), all while scapegoating past ancestors for the very same behavior (verse 25). In a textbook case of misdirection, the Nephites distract attention from their own sins by professing horror at the sins of others, whether Lamanites (as we saw in Hel. 4) or their own forefathers. In either case, the truth is the same: "Behold ye are worse than they" (13:26). Most alarmingly, Samuel implies that money corrupts the people's ability to identify true prophets. The only prophets the people receive are those who tell them what they want to hear, encouraging them to "do whatsoever [their] heart desireth" (verse 27). And because Nephite desires are dominated by affluence, they reward their false prophets in similar terms: "Ye will lift him up, and . . . give unto him of your gold, . . . and ye will clothe him with costly apparel" (verse 28). Having publicly justified the people in their refusal to examine the darkest, most invisible corners of their heart, these counterfeit prophets are fittingly rewarded in hypervisible, ostentatious fashion.

Unfortunately, because critiques of wealth are such a regular feature of scripture, it's easy for them to become a blur. Samuel's sermon challenges readers to be more self-critical. Are we not all Nephites, in the end? Are we not overly prone to rely on our bank accounts or our 401k to provide stability for tomorrow? Do we not all participate in an economy whose focus on accumulating money risks complicity in the "envyings, strifes, malice, [and] persecutions" (verse 22) that so often accompany corporate interests? We justify constraints on charitable giving far more regularly than we justify constraints on frivolous spending. We eliminate low-income housing and restrict zoning in our neighborhoods, letting homelessness and poverty go unaddressed in exchange for insulated property values or a few more percentage points of profit for developers. We howl over price increases far more earnestly than we lament over the difficulty of living on minimum wage. And then, to top it all off, we flock to the voices that assure us that our economic insularity is fine—voices that let us off the hook for prioritizing our financial security, that assuage the sting of ethical critique by assuring us that it's a corrupt *system* and what else could we have done, really? Any honest assessment of life in the twenty-first century must admit: our grip on our money is much harder to loosen than our grip on virtually any other part of our lives. We are often no better than the Nephites on this score, and we are just as liable to privilege voices that alleviate our guilt rather than stir us up to repentance. If scripture's prophets begin to sound boorish or repetitive on this point, it is only because we are as blind and self-congratulatory as the Nephites.

That blindness, Samuel hastens to point out, does not affect only its perpetrators. The Nephites have not only excluded certain sins and doctrines from their field of vision, but they've overlooked certain *people* as well. The first group is found surprisingly close to home: "And now, my beloved brethren, behold, . . . except ye shall repent your houses shall be left unto you desolate. Yea, except ye repent, your women shall have great cause to mourn" (15:1–2). Samuel here singles out the experiences and feelings of a specific group of people—Nephite women. In the coming day of destruction, he explains, "there shall be no place for refuge" for nursing mothers; indeed, "them which are with child . . . shall be heavy and cannot flee; therefore, they shall be trodden down and shall be left to perish" (verse 2). In their calculus of wealth-building, the Nephites have forgotten to account not only for the destruction that awaits the wicked but also for how much worse that destruction will impact their most vulnerable members. Nephite men, it seems, have failed to consider their families—failed to see their wives and the struggles of motherhood and the effects of economic greed on the domestic relationships that lie invisibly beneath the public world of markets and political power. Samuel funds his warning with characteristically vivid images: pregnant bodies littering the ground and nursing infants crying on a battlefield. The fecundity of mothers and the potential of young lives are crushed in a brutal metaphor of the Nephites' disregard for their own future. Though it is never comfortable to be confronted with one's wickedness or its consequences for the lives of loved ones, this is the horrifying image the Nephites must contemplate if there's any chance to avoid seeing it realized.

But this is not the only familial relationship the Nephites have overlooked, nor is it the only marginal group of people described in this chapter as being "trodden down" or "having no place for refuge" (verses 9, 12). These same descriptors are also applied to the

Lamanites, another persistent blind spot for Samuel's audience. In sharp contrast to the people's prejudice against their dark-skinned brothers, Samuel hastens to point out: "the more part of them [the Lamanites]...do walk circumspectly before God" (verse 5). Just as the Nephites have overlooked the plights of their women, they've also overlooked the true character of the Lamanites and thereby misunderstood God's covenant work: "In the latter times the promises of the Lord have been extended to our brethren, the Lamanites;...that they shall again be brought to the true knowledge...of their Redeemer" (verses 12–13). While the Nephites bedeck their false prophets in gold, a true prophet emerges from among the Lamanites, delivering the word of God in plainness. The people will soon bury treasures to secure a wealthy future for themselves, failing to appreciate that the Lamanites instead "buried their weapons of war" (verse 9) in order to secure a clear conscience at the judgment bar. And where the Lamanites just a few years before found themselves enjoying the company of angels and being encircled in heavenly fire, the Nephites instead, warns Samuel, risk destructive "fire...out of heaven" (13:13) and are "encircled about by the angels of him who hath sought to destroy our souls" (verse 37). "I would that ye should *behold*" these things, Samuel pleads; "ye can *see* that they fear to sin" and "ye can *see* of yourselves" the Lamanites' righteous resolve (15:5, 9, 15; emphasis added). Over and over, Samuel begs the people to find new eyes and to look in the directions to which God himself attends: domestic relationships, covenant promises, and the marginal identities that render his children socially invisible and unduly burdened.

With his eyes rightly trained, however, Samuel can also see what the Lamanites possess that the Nephites lack: *firmness*. Unlike the children of Nephi, the

Lamanites are "firm and steadfast in the faith" whenever it has been delivered to them (verse 8). They exhibit such "steadfastness" (verse 10), in fact, that the Nephites are roundly condemned by comparison: "Had the mighty works been shown unto them which have been shown unto you,...they never would again have dwindled in unbelief" (verse 15). In a book full of slippery treasures, an unsteady earth, and Nephite morality in a constant tailspin, the Lamanites are virtually the only immovable thing within these pages. Their firmness is so extreme, in fact, that it has secured for them a fixed promise from the Lord: "Because of their firmness...behold, the Lord shall...prolong their days" (verse 10). It is precisely through this exemplary faithfulness, in other words, that the Lamanites secure the covenant future that the Nephites are in the process of forfeiting.

Readers might draw two lessons from Samuel's Lamanite identity and his attention to the Lamanites in Helaman 15. First, this chapter reminds us that sometimes it takes an outsider to deliver God's voice. Nephi$_2$ also preached repentance to the Nephites, delivered an oracle of destruction, and prophesied of Christ, but he was too well known and too entangled in the local concerns of Zarahemla. Because Samuel stands free of the people's political tussles, he can present those same truths uninhibited. Unfortunately, Samuel is in some ways *too much* of an outsider: "And now, because I am a Lamanite,...ye are angry with me and...have cast me out from among you" (14:10). The Nephites will accept God's word from other mouths, it seems, but not from his. Had the Nephites exercised more care, they would have remembered that God's voice often issues from surprising corners and unexpected faces, and that sometimes outsiders make the best mirrors. What could contemporary Church members learn about their blind spots from nonmembers? What is reflected back to us by those not caught up in our insular concerns? Preaching, as Samuel so clearly exemplifies, need not always run in one direction only.

Second, Samuel reveals something readers have largely overlooked in their interpretation of the Book of Mormon: the Lamanites! Samuel is nothing like the Lamanites we've come to know and expect when presented through Nephite eyes. When women in the Book of Mormon are shown exercising political authority, acting with autonomy in their households, and even speaking in tongues, it occurs among the Lamanites (Alma 19). The Book of Mormon's most cosmic and precise prophecy of the Messiah comes, as we'll see in a moment, from a Lamanite (Hel. 14). The Lamanites also provide the Book of Mormon's best models for nonmilitary methods of achieving peace (Alma 24) and for rightly ordered domestic relationships (Jacob 2:35; 3:5–7). The most miraculous nationwide conversions, the most famous and faithful band of soldiers (Alma 53), and even the famous "remnant" to whom the Book of Mormon itself is addressed—all belong to the Lamanites. They have their moments of wickedness too, to be sure, but when they get it right, they get it far *more* right than the Nephites ever did.

In sum, the Nephites are doubly sightless: blind to their own sin and blind to the oppression they heap on the vulnerable around them. We, too, need less grasping after money and more firmness in the Lord, less seeking after our own interests and more regard for the lives around us; we need to be less like the Nephites, in short, and much, *much* more like the Lamanites in the book of Helaman. Here the Lamanites show readers how self-examination leads to repentance, how firmness obtains blessings from the Lord, and how closely God attends to the marginalized. Indeed, it is at the margins of Nephite attention that we will find the real arbiters of the covenant: homes and families, dark-skinned remnants, and the records that help us see these better.

*Samuel's signs and the problem with knowledge*

The Nephites are sightless in another way as well: they are blind to the Messiah. Sandwiched between Helaman 13's critique of wealth and Helaman 15's attention to women and Lamanites is Helaman 14's prophecy of the coming Christ. Curiously, Samuel opens this section not by announcing the Messiah directly but by announcing something that will make the Messiah's arrival visible: "Behold, I give unto you a sign" (14:2). There then follow two omens—one of Christ's birth and one of Christ's death—framing a brief digression on the nature of redemption. The Messiah's birth will be marked, Samuel reports, by roughly three days of miraculous light (verses 3–4), while his death will herald roughly three days of miraculous darkness (verse 20).

Samuel's signs are truly unparalleled in the Book of Mormon. Unlike Nephi$_2$, who used local agricultural mishaps and earth-bound political events to illustrate Nephite sin, Samuel presents signs that are cosmic in scale and apocalyptic in flavor, marking world-historical events. Nor does Samuel deliver these signs as one-time, isolable events; he also mentions "a new star" (verse 5) and many other "signs and wonders in heaven" (verse 6). Furthermore, Samuel's signs are notably nonpunitive, unlike most other cases of sign-giving in the Book of Mormon where signs demonstrate the falsity of an anti-Christ (Jacob 7:14–15; Alma 30:43–50) or convince an antagonistic audience of a prophet's credentials (Hel. 9:24–25). Rather than being punitive or evidentiary, Samuel's signs instead prioritize visibility. They deal with the sun, moon, and stars—hyperevident heavenly bodies whose luminescence and obvious course through the sky order day-to-day life. Furthermore, Samuel enlists these celestial objects explicitly for the purpose of rendering something perceptible. "I give you a sign," he says, because something "cometh" in five years: the Son of God (14:2). The Messiah's advent is devotionally invisible to these faithless Nephites, rationally invisible to a world that has never known a deity becoming mortal, and geographically invisible to Lehi₁ and Sariah's children living on a far-distant continent. Samuel's signs, then, help them look in the right direction by giving them something on which they can literally train their eyes.

But not just any glance will do. Because Samuel's signs have a very specific object—Christ himself—they also operate in a very specific way. To be precise, the two signs work in concert to draw attention to the messianic life that sits between them. The excessive light around Christ's birth and the excessive darkness around Christ's death almost serve as two halves of the same sign, as if they were a kind of single, cosmic day. The miraculous light that attends Christ's entry to the world signals all the hope and optimism human beings associate with daybreak, while the thick darkness at the Savior's death reminds us of the finality and closure we associate with nightfall. In this way, rather than designating Christ's birth and death as isolable events with discrete salvific import, Samuel's signs bookend Christ's entire ministry. The sun rises and sets on the Lord's sojourn with man. Samuel doesn't simply direct the Nephites to two specific moments in Christ's life; rather, the signs work together to gesture toward the whole person and life suspended between them.

But these signs are not meant to correct only for physical distance. The Nephites' blindness regarding the Messiah is more a matter of faithlessness than it is of geographic realities. Luckily, Samuel has a remedy to this faithlessness as well—or, at least, the chance of one. Tucked in among his announcement in Helaman 14 is Samuel's instruction to listeners about how these signs are meant to work on viewers' hearts. He begins in verse 11 with a somewhat surprising relationship between knowledge and belief:

> For this intent have I come up upon the walls of this city, that ye might hear and know of the judgments of God which do await you because of your iniquities, and also that ye might know the conditions of repentance; and also that ye might know of the coming of Jesus Christ, the Son of God, . . . and that ye might know of the *signs* of his coming, to the intent that ye might believe on his name. (verses 11–12; emphasis added)

Samuel gives the Nephites a mountain of knowledge about God and Christ and redemption, hoping they will find belief at its summit. Besides reversing our usual intuition that faith leads to knowledge rather than the other way around, Samuel does something else rather curious in these verses. Notice that he inserts "signs" between the verses' last mention of knowledge and the belief he hopes these signs will inspire. It is signs, according to Samuel, that will transition his listeners from knowledge to faith. This should strike contemporary readers as odd. After all, aren't signs and visibility usually contrasted with belief? Signs follow faith (Mark 16:17), scripture teaches, and faith is a matter of "things which are not seen" (Alma 32:21). How can Samuel privilege faith over knowledge, and how can he say, of all things, that visible signs will *lead* to faith?

Two clues in surrounding verses might help. First, Samuel adds a few clarifying details in verse 28:

> Many shall see greater [signs] than these, to the intent that they *might* believe that these signs and these wonders should come to pass...to the intent that there should be *no cause for unbelief* among the children of men. (Hel. 14:28; emphasis added)

As in verse 12, readers are reminded that signs produce only the *potential* for belief rather than compelling belief automatically; signs are given so the people only "might" believe. Miraculous omens cannot force faith, in other words, but they can create conditions where faith is possible. But as soon as Samuel reiterates that point, he specifies further: signs are a matter of preventing "cause for *un*belief"—they thwart something negative rather than straightforwardly causing something positive. Signs, Samuel teaches, create the conditions for faith by fending off the conditions for unbelief. They cannot compel faith where faith is lacking, but they may create space for a kernel of faith to grow more freely.

Our second clue takes us back to the mechanics of Samuel's first sign, where we find another mention of knowledge:

> Therefore, there shall be one day and a night and a day, as if it were one day...for ye shall know of the rising of the sun and also of its setting; therefore they shall know of a surety that there shall be two days and a night; nevertheless the night shall not be darkened. (verse 4; emphasis added)

106

Samuel describes what the Nephites will "know" at the time of this sign. This miraculous daylight, which persists through the evident rising and setting of the sun, will challenge the Nephites' knowledge—not because the sign denies it outright but because their knowledge is insufficient to understand the situation in which they will find themselves. With the first sign, the people will see the sun setting and rising, and yet the world around them will remain illuminated as if it were high noon. The second sign also thwarts their sight, though in a different way; in this case, everything will be dark and shaking—their eyes won't function here (verses 20–21). Samuel's signs show the Nephites the frailty of their sight and the insufficiency of their knowledge. They clear the ground for faith by unsettling Nephite confidence that they know how the world works and that they are intellectual masters of a situation. Though there is never a perfect overlap between our perspective and reality, signs can render that gap newly visible. Indeed, Samuel's signs reveal the size of that gap to be much larger than the Nephites tend to imagine.

For Samuel, then, faith is neither a stepping-stone on the way to certainty nor the starting line of our spiritual race. On the contrary, verse 11 positions knowledge as the starting line because, quite frankly, we are far more awash in knowledge than we are in faith. The Nephites, for instance, know all too well how the sun moves through the sky and how to forecast the remaining daylight; what they lack is faith that these natural phenomena can be overturned. They are familiar with centuries of Lamanite rivalry and wickedness; they need to glimpse instead that Lamanite repentance is nevertheless a real possibility. The people are well acquainted with the unlikelihood of a divine Messiah being born on a foreign continent; what they fail to

107

see is that this miracle might be just five years away. Like the Nephites, we too have plenty of knowledge—we've been acquiring knowledge since the day we were born. Many of us have been blessed with public school educations and college degrees and vocational training. We know reams of information about the world and our place in it. Faith, however, means looking for how the world can change beyond—or even in spite of—what we know. It means cultivating a sense that we live on the cusp of divine possibilities that could break in at any moment and unsettle our tired patterns and empty certainties. We may start with knowledge, in other words, but it is not the end goal, and signs can be a route to faith, Samuel implies, if they encourage us to hold that knowledge a little more lightly.

*aftermath*

Despite such clear-eyed appraisal of their sin, the Nephites still squirm out of their chance. Samuel's sermon comes to a close, the crowd starts hurling rocks, and he disappears into the wilderness and off the pages of the Book of Mormon (Hel. 16:2, 6–7). Or, rather, he "did flee out of their lands...even unto his own country and began to preach and to prophesy among his own people" [verse 7]. His words effect repentance in a few (verses 1, 3–5), but for the most part there is "little alteration in the affairs of the people" (verse 12). The Nephites spend the next several years solidifying their wickedness: where the Lamanites exhibit firmness, the Nephites instead grow "hardened" (verse 12). Clamping down on their view of the world and clinging to their assumptions, the people become rigid and unyielding. It is thus little surprise that, once signs begin to appear (verse 13), the people "harden their hearts . . . [and] depend . . . upon their own wisdom" (verse 15). Despite Samuel's hope that signs might prompt the Nephites to loosen their grip on their certainties, the people show no hint of altering their ways.

Their rigidity begins, as all self-delusion does, with internal dialogue. As prophecy begins to be fulfilled in the years immediately following Samuel's sermon, Mormon gives us a sample of Nephite reasoning: "Some things they may have guessed right, among so many," the people scoff, "but behold, we know that all these great and marvelous works cannot come to pass" (verse 16). In the gap between "some" and "all," the Nephites begin to play a probability game. They admit that "some" signs have occurred but profess confidence that "all" the prophecies cannot possibly come to pass. Instead of revising their hypotheses or feeling spurred to critical self-reflection, the people spend their intellectual energy explaining the signs away as mere prophetic guesswork. Forging ahead in their self-assurance, the Nephites also "began to reason . . . among themselves, saying: that it is not reasonable that such a being as a Christ shall come" (verses 17–18). Inverting Samuel's earlier model of knowledge and faith, the people persist in a dangerous overvaluation of "reason." They prefer a worldview that grants them intellectual security and control rather than enduring the spiritual growth that follows admissions of uncertainty or ignorance. Knowledge can give way to faith, Samuel taught, when it is supplemented with invisible possibilities and made subject to revision. The Nephites, however, would rather stick to knowledge alone and then pat themselves on the back for being clear-eyed realists.

The problem, here, is not with the Nephites' insistence on rationality. On the contrary, scripture encourages readers to pair faith with study (D&C 88:118) and our commitment to the compatibility of faith and knowledge is evident in every testimony that begins with the words "I know." No, the Nephites' problem is what lies *hidden* by their insistence on rationality. Indeed, there are hints that the Nephites are far from the good-faith rationalists they make themselves out to be. Notice, first, the thinly veiled hubris that lies behind the words "we know" in Helaman 16:16. The people insist they *know* that all the prophecies cannot be fulfilled—not "we suspect" or "experience suggests" or "it seems to us..." Truly earnest thinkers would acknowledge the unknowability of the future and admit at least a slight margin for error in their assessments; instead, the Nephites stubbornly refuse any possibility that they might be wrong. They are professing total certainty about the future—something that is, quite obviously, impossible for human beings to have. If the people were merely trying to give a rational description of the world or a logical explanation for why these signs do not compel them to faith, they would not speak in such absolute terms. The fact that they admit no uncertainty suggests they are not engaged in an innocent descriptive project.

Looking ahead to their next assertion of knowledge, the people betray the real motivations behind their reasoning: "Behold, we know that this is a wicked tradition...which will keep us down to be...servants unto them" (Hel. 16: 20–21). The Nephites are on the lookout for power games. If something cannot be presented to their eyes for inspection, they insist, it must be suspect and underhanded. Readers who came to Helaman expecting endorsement for sleuthing out secret plots and hand-wringing over invisible exercises of power do find, at the very close of the book, an instance of that kind of thinking—but they find it among the wicked, not the righteous.

Furthermore, this combative worldview blinds the Nephites to the power game they themselves are playing. They are caught in the very same behavior of which they accuse the prophets, namely, exercising power over their religious opponents. By identifying the violence of others without also turning a self-critical eye to the same trends in their own thinking, the people find themselves on the side of real atrocities. Just one year later, readers witness these professed opponents of ideological coercion plotting a mass extermination of believers (3 Ne. 1:9). Though religion is certainly prone to power games, and though history is littered with examples of religious faith being used to persecute and oppress, that is not *all* that religion amounts to. By refusing to acknowledge the possibility that there is more than a power game at work, here, the people also overlook just how much dominance they attempt to exercise in return. Their readiness to explain religious phenomena as an expression of power reveals more about their own hunger for power, in this instance, than it does about the believers'.

Herein lies a final lesson about the danger of prioritizing knowledge over faith. By using their reasoning to play power games, justifying themselves in the assumption that this must also be what the other side is doing, the Nephites put their knowledge in the service of mastery rather than belief. If we are not careful, knowledge can become a tool for mastering other people rather than a tool for service or a good in its own right. There is a big difference between knowledge as testimony and knowledge as mastery. When our knowledge becomes an occasion for shaming others or a platform for grandstanding or a way of justifying ourselves in browbeating those who do not share our worldview, we can be sure that we are misusing it. To behave in these ways is to become like the unbelieving Nephites who, proudly proclaiming what they "know" to be true, talk themselves into smugness, self-congratulation, and persecution of others.

Because faith is a relationship to what lies beyond our sight, the Nephites ridicule it as mere guesswork. What they fail to understand, however, is that the invisibility of faith's object is not a lack or a weakness—it is the entire point. We focus on what is invisible not because we wish to escape into fantasy or fund a fretful search for unseen power moves. We focus on what is invisible because that's where potential lies. The world is always subject to revision, always on the cusp of change, and underwritten by an array of possibilities. We exercise faith to the precise degree that we supplement the evidence of our eyes with a sensitivity to the divine potential that can surprise us at any moment. Revelation can arrive out of the blue, enemy hearts can transform overnight, and God's power can turn back the very motion of the sun. Faith means relating to the "in the meantime" moments with trust that miracles might be just around the corner. Faith is a matter of unseen things not because we trust that everything invisible will one day submit itself to our point of view but because the whole realm of the visible is oriented by something—and Someone—that lies invisibly beyond it. And if faith is a question of what lies hidden in the far-off future or the distant heavens, it is also just as much a question of what lies hidden in the hearts of those around us. Whether it means attending to the concealed sorrows of our neighbor, the promise of a Messiah who is not yet here, or the whisperings of inspiration that do not register audibly on the ears, a life of faith always operates in light of what we cannot see.

# Conclusion

Writing to the early saints in Rome, Paul warned that "the wrath of God is revealed from heaven against all...who hold the truth in unrighteousness....For the invisible things of him from the creation of the world are clearly seen,...so that they are without excuse" (Rom. 1:18, 20). God's creation is rife with "invisible things" that should be "clearly seen"—truths that, in themselves, are perfectly evident and readily available to the eyes but that remain "invisible" only because we "hold" them in the wrong way. The Greek word behind verse 18 is especially damning: we don't just *hold* the truth wrongly, we "suppress" (*katechō*) it in unrighteousness. We censor and bury and scurry out of sight our greatest weaknesses and rationalize our favorite sins. We dull our own eyesight and bask in a blurry image of ourselves that obscures unnerving details around the margins. The result, according to Paul, is that God eventually leaves us to our preference: "Professing themselves to be wise, they became fools....Wherefore God gave them up to...the lusts of their own hearts" (1:22, 24). If we choose invisible suppression over divine clarity for long enough, we, like the Nephites, will be left alone with a fuzzy, idolatrous perspective on the world.

Our reading of the book of Helaman leaves us with an inescapable conclusion: you and I are wrong. Profoundly, devastatingly wrong about a great many things—many of them quite important. We hold incorrect assumptions, misinterpret the intentions of others, and accept as truths things that are not, in fact, true. Even more damningly, the book of Helaman suggests that, like the Nephites, we offload our errors onto the images we've constructed of others, pitting ourselves against a wicked "world" and convincing ourselves that we're the righteous ones. We traffic in prejudices against those who look and act differently and refuse the possibility that the word of God might be issuing to us from differently colored faces. We hide up treasures, trusting our futures to our bank accounts and the value of our equity. We trust that if our country, our state, our neighborhood looks fine, then all is well in Zion—ignoring, meanwhile, the cries of the poverty-stricken and oppressed outside the gates. Whatever the scope or kind of our blindness, we can be certain that somewhere in our lives there is a corner of our hearts that we've been only too happy to leave in shadow.

The book of Helaman encourages us to shed light on those invisible corners, to make a habit of self-critique, and to loosen our grip on our certainties. Even on the vanishingly rare occasions when we happen to be 100 percent correct, we almost certainly relate to that truth in the wrong way. Your confidence in the laws of physics may be warranted, but have you spun that confidence into contempt for others without your educational opportunities? You may fully understand the intentions of another person who has deliberately wronged you, but have you used that understanding to justify lingering resentments? Even our testimonies of the gospel are too easily converted into bludgeons against those whose lives take a different shape than our own. Genuine truths regularly become sites of petty emotions and sinful fantasies—not because the knowledge is wrong but because the knowers are human. The book of Helaman echoes loudly the words of King Benjamin: "This much I can tell you, that if ye do not watch yourselves, and your thoughts, and your words, and your deeds,...ye must perish" (Mosiah 4:30).

If we come away from our reading of Helaman shaking our heads at the blindness and willful stupidity of the Nephites, patting ourselves on the back for noticing what they failed to see, or eagerly sleuthing for secret enemies lurking in the shadows, we will have missed the message of this text. The message of Helaman is not "be hypervigilant against threat" but rather "you are not as good at assessing threats as you think you are." The book of Helaman encourages readers to turn a self-critical eye on themselves, their relationships, and their treasures; to look in the mirror of prophetic words to see where we fall short and where God is staring pointedly back at *us*; to excavate the invisible corners of our hearts and clear room for heaven to surprise us.

Discipleship is a matter of training our vision to view unflinchingly the truths about ourselves that we want most to bury and the realities about the world that we want most to avoid. Christ shied away from neither. He was a preacher of human weakness who spent his life relentlessly casting his gaze on the extremes of human sin and suffering and then training everyone around him to look their way as well. I trust that Christ's return will bring the same things into view that were rendered visible during his ministry. I trust, too, that his coming will not be a triumphant confirmation of all the ways I am right and everyone else is wrong. I am confident that at his coming we will be surprised. If scripture teaches us anything about God, it's that God always thwarts our expectations and shows us things we never could have anticipated. Indeed, it has been an unfailing truth in my life that genuine revelation inevitably comes as a surprise. Thank the heavens for a God of surprising sights; his work could not be a wonder without them.

# Further Reading

The thoughts in this book grow out of several years' previous research. For more of my work on Helaman 5, the role of Samuel the Lamanite, and the structure of Helaman, see:

Berkey, Kimberly. "Works of Darkness: Secret Combinations and Covenant Displacement in the Book of Mormon." In *Reading Nephi Reading Isaiah: Reading 2 Nephi 26–27*, edited by Joseph M. Spencer and Jenny Webb, 105–21. Provo, UT: Neal A. Maxwell Institute for Religious Scholarship, 2016.

———. "Temporality and Fulfillment in 3 Nephi 1." *Journal of Book of Mormon Studies* 24, no. 1 (2015): 53–83.

———. "Narrative Doubling and the Structure of Helaman." *Journal of Book of Mormon Studies* 28 (2019): 69–90.

For a representative sample of Latter-day Saint perspectives on the book of Helaman in the late twentieth century, see:

Nyman, Monte S., and Charles D. Tate, Jr., eds. *The Book of Mormon: Helaman through 3 Nephi 8, According to Thy Word*. Provo, UT: BYU Religious Studies Center, 1992.

On Samuel the Lamanite and his role in the Book of Mormon's metacritique of theological racism, see:

Hickman, Jared. "*The Book of Mormon* as Amerindian Apocalypse." *American Literature* 86, no. 3 (2014): 429–61.

For one of the best theological treatments of Samuel's sermon, attending specifically to the question of temporality, see:

Spencer, Joseph M. "The Time of Sin." *Interpreter* 9 (2014): 87–110.

For more on the use of the phrase "as if" in the Book of Mormon, including a parallel account of its role specifically in Helaman 5, see:

Turley, Kylie Nielson. "(Unreal) Fire and (Faithless) Sincerity: The Impact of 'As If' in Helaman 5." Paper presented at the Book of Mormon Studies Association conference, Logan, UT, October 12, 2019.

———. *Alma 1–29: a brief theological introduction*. Provo, UT: Neal A. Maxwell Institute for Religious Scholarship, 2020.

On the historical impact of the book of Helaman among Latter-day Saints, see:

Reeve, W. Paul. "'As Ugly as Evil' and 'as Wicked as Hell': Gadianton Robbers and the Legend Process among the Mormons." *Journal of Mormon History* 27, no. 2 (2001): 125–49.

Mason, Patrick Q. "Ezra Taft Benson and Modern (Book of) Mormon Conservatism." In *Out of Obscurity: Mormonism since 1945*, edited by Patrick Q. Mason and John G. Turner, 63–80. New York: Oxford University Press, 2016.

# Index

**124**

**126**

# Colophon

The text of the book is typeset in Arnhem,
Fred Smeijer's 21st-century-take on late
18th-century Enlightenment-era letterforms
known for their sturdy legibility and clarity
of form. Captions and figures are typset in
Quaadraat Sans, also by Fred Smeijers.
The book title and chapter titles are typeset
in Thema by Nikola Djurek.

Printed on Domtar Lynx 74 gsm,
Forest Stewardship Council (FSC) Certified.

Printed by Brigham Young University Print & Mail Services

Woodcut illuminations **Brian Kershisnik**
Illumination consultation **Faith Heard**

Book design & typography **Douglas Thomas**
Production typesetting **Natalie Miles, Sage Perez, Maria Camargo**
Chart design **Sage Perez, Douglas Thomas**

Helaman 5:48 And now, when they heard this they cast up their eyes as if to behold from whence the voice came; and behold, they saw the heavens open; and angels came down out of heaven and ministered unto them.